THEODORE ROOSEVELT
for Kids

HIS LIFE AND TIMES ❖ 21 ACTIVITIES

KERRIE LOGAN HOLLIHAN

**CHICAGO
REVIEW
PRESS**

To my father, Frederick D. Logan, who drove my family through the Theodore Roosevelt National Park in a 1961 Chevy station wagon.

Library of Congress Cataloging-in-Publication Data

Hollihan, Kerrie Logan.

Theodore Roosevelt for kids : his life and times, 21 activities / Kerrie Logan Hollihan. — 1st ed.

p. cm.

Includes index.

ISBN 978-1-55652-955-9 (pbk.)

1. Roosevelt, Theodore, 1858-1919—Juvenile literature.   2. Presidents—United States—Biography—Juvenile literature.   3. Creative activities and seat work—Juvenile literature.   I. Title.

E757.H646 2010

973.911092—dc22

[B]

2009048060

Cover and interior design: Monica Baziuk

Interior illustrations: Laura D'Argo

Cover images: Roosevelt children: Sagamore Hill National Historical Site, National Park Service / Grand Canyon and teddy bear: Shutterstock / Theodore Roosevelt in suit, Medal of Honor, Roosevelt on horseback, meatpacking plant, Panama Canal, and Rough Riders: Library of Congress

First edition

Published by Chicago Review Press, Incorporated

814 North Franklin Street

Chicago, Illinois 60610

ISBN 978-1-55652-955-9

Printed in the United States of America

5   4   3   2   1

It is not the critic who counts, not the man who points out how the strong man stumbled, or where the doer of deeds could have done them better. The credit belongs to the man who is actually in the arena; whose face is marred by dust and sweat and blood; who strives valiantly; who errs and comes short again and again; who knows the great enthusiasms, the great devotions, and spends himself in a worthy cause.

—Theodore Roosevelt

Contents

Time Line

October 27, 1858	Theodore Roosevelt is born to Theodore Roosevelt Sr. and Martha Bulloch Roosevelt in New York City.
April 1865	Theodore Roosevelt and his parents view Abraham Lincoln's funeral procession.
1869–1870	The Roosevelt family makes its grand tour of Europe.
1872–1873	The Roosevelts make their second grand tour including Egypt, Palestine, and Greece.
1876	Roosevelt begins his freshman year at Harvard College.
1878	Roosevelt's father dies.
1880	Roosevelt graduates with top honors from Harvard College and enters Columbia Law School.
October 27, 1880	Roosevelt marries Alice Lee on his 22nd birthday.
November 1881	Roosevelt is elected to New York State Assembly as he leaves law school.
1883–1884	Roosevelt buys two cattle ranches in North Dakota's Badlands.
February 12, 1884	Alice Lee Roosevelt is born to Theodore and Alice.
February 14, 1884	Roosevelt's mother and wife die on the same day.
Summer 1884	Roosevelt moves to his ranch in the Badlands.
November 1886	Roosevelt is defeated in an election for mayor of New York City.

December 2, 1886	Roosevelt marries Edith Kermit Carow.
September 1887	Theodore Roosevelt (known as Theodore Roosevelt Jr.) is born to Theodore and Edith.
May 1889–May 1895	Roosevelt serves as civil service commissioner, Washington D.C.
October 1889	Kermit Roosevelt is born.
August 1891	Ethel Carow Roosevelt is born.
1894	Archibald Bulloch Roosevelt is born.
May 1895–April 1897	Roosevelt serves as president of the Board of Police Commissioners, New York City.
April 1897	Roosevelt serves as assistant secretary of the navy.
November 1897	Theodore's sixth child, Quentin Roosevelt, is born.
May 1898	Roosevelt becomes lieutenant-colonel of the Rough Riders.
July 1, 1898	Roosevelt leads the Rough Riders in the Battle of San Juan Heights.
January 2, 1899	Roosevelt is inaugurated as governor of New York.
November 6, 1900	Roosevelt is elected vice president of the United States.
September 6, 1901	President William McKinley is shot by an assassin.
September 14, 1901	Roosevelt becomes 26th president of the United States.
November 8, 1904	Roosevelt is elected to a second term as president.
March 4, 1909	Roosevelt leaves the White House and goes on safari.
1912	Roosevelt runs as third-party Progressive candidate for president.
1914	Roosevelt nearly dies during Amazon expedition.
1916	Roosevelt turns down Progressive Party nomination for president.
1917	President Woodrow Wilson denies Roosevelt's request to serve in World War I.
January 6, 1919	Theodore Roosevelt dies in his sleep at Sagamore Hill.

Preface

The Once and Future President

President Theodore Roosevelt wore strands of Abraham Lincoln's hair in this ring at his second inauguration in 1905.

Sagamore Hill National Historic Site, National Park Service

ON THE afternoon of April 24, 1865, a family gathered for a sorry task at the home of its leading member, Cornelius Roosevelt. Grandfather Roosevelt's windows overlooked Broadway, one of New York City's main streets. As the Roosevelts and their friends crowded to watch at the windows, a funeral procession passed below.

The parade wound on for blocks as 11,000 military men and another 75,000 ordinary citizens walked by. They marched to honor the man whose coffin was pulled by a team of 16 black-robed horses. The dead man was President Abraham Lincoln. Ten days before, an assassin had shot and killed him.

Two Roosevelts who peered out the windows were small boys, Theodore and Elliott. Theodore, whose family called him Teedie, was six and a half years old. President Lincoln was his hero. Lincoln had just won the Civil War, when the Union fought against the Confederate South to preserve the United States of America as one nation.

No one looking out of Grandfather Roosevelt's windows could guess that, 36 years from that afternoon, Theodore would be president of the United States. Nor did they know that as he took the presidential oath of office for a second time, Theodore Roosevelt would wear strands of Abraham Lincoln's hair in a ring on his right hand.

Theodore and Elliott Roosevelt watch from the second-floor window of their grandfather's home as Abraham Lincoln's funeral procession passes below.

Sagamore Hill National Historic Site, National Park Service

1

Teedie

IN THE dark hours of night in the mid-1860s, a gas lamp flared in an upstairs room. There, in bed, a small boy sat up gasping. Asthma had attacked him, and he could not breathe.

The little boy's father, a wealthy New Yorker, ordered servants to the livery stable nearby. The father scooped up his son, bundled him warmly, and carried him downstairs and outside. In moments, a carriage and horses appeared. The father got in and placed the little boy beside him. Taking the reins himself, the father flicked his whip and urged his horses into action.

The open carriage rumbled down the Manhattan streets through the fresh night air. Block after block they drove as the little boy wheezed, trying to catch his breath. Then more miles to travel, the horses clopping a steady, calming beat, until the little boy's gasps gave way to puffs and finally gulps as air filled his lungs.

Teedie Roosevelt could breathe.

Again, his father had come to his aid, as only a boy's father could. To Teedie, his father seemed like the strong-minded Great-Heart, whom he had read about in a book called *Pilgrim's Progress*.

Teedie's name was Theodore Roosevelt, just like his father's. Theodore Roosevelt Sr. was one of New York's leading citizens, the seventh Roosevelt to make his home on the island of Manhattan. The family had its roots in Holland, and its members pronounced their name in the same way the flower is pronounced. "Roosevelt" means "field of roses."

Teedie's mother, Martha Bulloch Roosevelt, came from a different background. Mittie, as her family knew her, hailed from the Deep South, a rural culture of large plantations and smaller farms. Like many farmers—rich or not—the Bulloch family depended on their African American slaves to grow their crops and work in their homes.

Teedie's parents married in 1853, and his mother became mistress of their New York brownstone home. In less than a year, their first child arrived. They named her Anna but called her Bamie (rhyming with Tammy).

Then, on October 27, 1858, their first son was born. Soon the little boy had his pet name: Teedie. The house at 28 East Twentieth Street filled quickly with more children— Elliott (called Ellie) in 1860 and Corinne (Conie) in 1861.

As a small child, Teedie heard grownups talk about the Civil War and its furious battles between North and South. Teedie was three when the war began in 1861. By the time it ended in 1865, he was six and a half and firmly for the Union, like his father. In the Roosevelt home, however, there was little war talk. Mittie's mother and sister lived with the Roosevelts. The three Southern ladies fretted about Mittie's two brothers, who fought in the Confederate States Navy.

There could have been arguments about the war in the Roosevelt home, but there were none. Teedie's father, out of respect for Mittie's family, hired a substitute to fight for him in the Union Army. Such payments were common among elite families in the North during the Civil War. America's very wealthy families did not take part in politics. The dirty wrangling of political life, they felt, was below them. Nor did they fight in battle.

Nonetheless, Teedie watched as his father reached out to families of soldiers. The wives and children of Union soldiers were going hungry. Teedie's father had a plan for soldiers

to send part of their pay home. His father left New York to spend weeks in Washington, D.C. In time, his father persuaded President Abraham Lincoln to approve his idea.

In letters to his father, Mittie wrote about how sick Teedie was. The little boy had his first asthma attack when he was three. He suffered so badly that he spent much of his childhood in bed. Doctors in his day had little to offer. At one point they suggested that puffing on a cigar might stop an attack. Teedie could not go to school, so the Roosevelts hired tutors to educate him at home.

Teedie's delicate condition could not keep him from learning. Once he learned to read, there was no stopping him. Copies of *Our Young Folks*, a children's magazine, poured into the Roosevelt home, and Teedie devoured them all. He also read "The Saga of King Olaf," a poem by Henry Wadsworth Longfellow. From then on, stories of the Nordic heroes of Scandinavia captivated him.

Newspaper stories about the adventures of Dr. David Livingstone, the great English explorer to Africa, excited Teedie as well. He dreamed about tracking his way through uncharted lands in search of exotic animals and unnamed rivers. Sometimes Teedie sneaked dime novels into the house, cheap books that his parents prohibited because they felt they were trashy and kids shouldn't read them.

MAKE A "PIGSKIN" NOTEBOOK

TEEDIE ROOSEVELT jotted down his observations from an early age and kept a journal. Books and journals often were bound in pigskin, a waterproof material. You can create your own "pigskin" journal and use it to make notes and drawings.

You'll Need

❖ Masking tape
❖ Scissors
❖ Tape-bound composition notebook
❖ Newspaper
❖ Rubber gloves
❖ Soft rag
❖ Brown shoe polish

To begin, cut strips of masking tape about 2 inches long and place them along the edge of the table where you are working.

Now cover both sides of the composition notebook with the strips of tape. Overlap the strips so that they create an uneven, leather-like look. Trim the edges of the tape flush with the edges of the notebook. Keep working until you have the look you like!

Open a newspaper and spread it out to cover your work area. Put on the rubber gloves. Dip the rag into the shoe polish and use it to dye the masking tape brown. You might need to do this several times until you get the depth of color you like. Let the polish dry between coats.

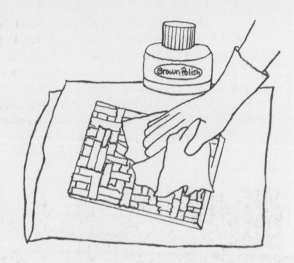

Now you are ready to do the rest of the activities in this book!

Early on, Teedie showed unusual curiosity about the natural world. On a morning trip to the market, he passed a butcher's stall where he spotted a dead seal. Teedie had read about seals in books, and here lay one for him to see. Every day he returned to look at the animal and brought along a folding ruler to measure it. Bit by bit, however, the meat was sold to customers, but the enterprising Teedie managed to bring the seal's skull home.

Teedie added the skull to the "Roosevelt Museum of Natural History" in his bedroom. When a housemaid complained, the "museum" found a new spot on shelves in a faraway part of the house. "It was the ordinary small boy's collection of curios," he wrote years later, but it kept him busy for hours.

Teedie started a notebook to keep track of his "ofserv-a-tions" of insects and fish. Whenever the weather turned warm, the Roosevelts left New York for spots in the country. There Teedie could wander about searching for crayfish, eels, "beetlles," and "misqueto" hawks. He kept notes faithfully, though his spelling needed work.

Teedie probably did not realize that his mother took him to the country to stop his attacks from asthma. The four children loved their days at Tranquility, a house on Long Island's Oyster Bay where their Roosevelt grandparents summered. Often cousins and friends joined them, including one of Corinne's closest playmates, a little girl named Edith Carow. The girls welcomed Teedie to join in because he played games of Store and Baby. In time, Teedie grew old enough to have a little rowboat of his own, and he named it for Edith.

A Victorian Childhood

THE ROOSEVELT children grew up under the strict customs of their day. "Victorian" ways ruled families in the mid-1800s, both in Europe and the Americas. The times got their name from Victoria, queen of the United Kingdom of Great Britain and Ireland, who ruled an empire around the globe.

The Victorians moved in a world with firm ideas about society. People divided themselves into classes according to their income and education. Middle-class men and women worked in separate spheres: men out earning an income, women at home running their households and caring for their children. Things were similar on America's farms. Men did the heavy work in the fields and cared for livestock. Wives kept house, raised chickens, and cultivated vegetable gardens.

Victorians claimed to hold high ideals, at least in public. They followed strict rules about manners. Physical punishment was common in school and at home. "Spare the

Theodore Roosevelt as a small boy. Theodore Roosevelt Birthplace National Historic Site, National Park Service

rod and spoil the child," Victorians declared. Husbands were expected to rule their wives, and fathers ruled their families. Children were expected to obey their parents, never to talk back.

This was an era when most little children wore baby dresses until the boys were old enough to wear pants. (Teedie didn't wear pants until he was five.) Girls never wore pants. Parents thought about boyhood or girlhood, and how their children would develop into adults, but the word "teenager" didn't exist.

In any case, everyone stayed covered during these times when modesty was key. Girls did not wear long skirts until they neared womanhood, but pantalettes hid their legs. Men wore hats and ladies wore bonnets.

Even furniture was covered up. Proper Victorian ladies covered the "limbs" of their sofas and pianos with heavy drapes. Certain matters were never discussed in mixed company of gentlemen and ladies. When a lady was clearly pregnant, she stayed at home and did not go out. To be sure, there was no talk of where babies came from.

Sundays stood apart from the rest of the week. In the Roosevelt house, it was a day for going to church—sometimes twice—with the rest of the time spent in quiet thinking. No loud games, no wild play—those were the rules. Teedie disliked Sundays. (A historian

BUILD A COLLECTION

TEEDIE ROOSEVELT'S curiosity about nature led him to become an avid collector. Building a collection is a fun way to become an expert on a subject that especially interests you.

You can collect all kinds of things—rocks, shells, toy cars, insects, stamps, dolls, or baseball cards. The collections can be more unusual—keys of all sorts, cicada shells, empty cheese crisp bags, or squares of toilet paper from bathrooms all over the world. Let your imagination soar! But before you stray too far from reality, it's wise to think about some other points.

How will you build your collection? Will you find items easily in your own neighborhood? Or will you need to add things as you go places with your family?

How will you display your collection? Thinking about how to store and exhibit your collection is one of the fun parts. Can you build a simple set of shelves with blocks and boards? Egg cartons make great storage and display cases for small items, and so do empty shoe boxes that you stack and tape together.

What's your budget? Some collections are inexpensive to start, but collecting things like rare coins, old stamps, or vintage toy airplanes can start to make a dent in your wallet. You'll need to think carefully about anything you buy and how to pay for it.

How will you organize, label, and catalog your treasures? There are lots of ways to set up a collection. Take rocks, for instance. You can organize by size, by color (red, white, pink, black, speckled), by name (crystal, quartz, limestone, granite), by type (sedimentary, metamorphic, igneous), or by location (where you picked them up).

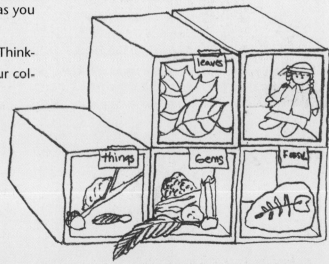

has pointed out that's when Teedie often had asthma attacks.)

Yet Sunday was the one day each week when Teedie and his siblings were allowed in the grand front parlor of their home, whose magnificent gas chandelier lit up the evening. The only other time the parlor opened was when guests arrived.

A Grand Tour

IN MAY 1869, when Teedie was 10, the Roosevelts set sail for Europe. To make the "Grand Tour" was a tradition for wealthy Americans. Only in Europe, they believed, could one experience true culture. Over the course of a year, the Roosevelts saw England, Germany, France, and Italy. Classy capital cities, great cathedrals, collections of fine art, ancient ruins—all were the order of the day.

Not for Teedie, however. It was still no fun having asthma attacks. He would have liked to stay home and work on his museum. He later wrote, "I cordially hated it, as did my younger brother and sister. Practically all the enjoyment we had was in exploring any ruins or mountains when we could get away from our elders, and in playing in the different hotels."

Teedie was overjoyed when the family returned home in May 1870. Summer, the best season of the year, lay ahead. There were

Teedie Roosevelt sits in his custom-made chair. After Teedie complained that horsehair furniture scratched his legs, his father ordered this one covered in soft red velvet. Sagamore Hill National Historic Site, National Park Service

pets to romp with and a Shetland pony named General Grant (after the great Union soldier Ulysses S. Grant, the future president). The children ran barefoot, "and the seasons went by in a round of . . . pleasures—supervising the haying and harvesting, picking apples, hunting frogs successfully and woodchucks unsuccessfully."

Sometimes the children "played Indians" and built wigwams in the woods, staining their skins with poke-cherry juice. They did not know any Indian children in person; what they knew about America's native peoples was through books they read and stories they heard.

The summer Teedie was 13, he received his first shotgun. Eagerly he took his first practice shots. But unlike his friends, he could not hit a thing. One of the boys pointed to a billboard off in the distance, and Teedie had a shock. "Not only was I unable to read the sign but I could not even see the letters."

Teedie was severely nearsighted; he had just never realized it. A word with his father and the problem was solved with a pair of eyeglasses. When he looked back on his boyhood, he mused, "I had no idea how beautiful the world was until I got those spectacles."

Now that Teedie could see, nature opened up even more to him. He began to learn taxidermy by stuffing the skins of animals and birds. Taxidermy was an art form among scientists of the day who collected specimens of wildlife in order to study them.

In Manhattan, Teedie's father helped to launch the American Museum of Natural History. The museum sent scientists on expeditions to the far corners of the earth. As specimens of animals and birds arrived back home, zoologists mounted them for study. Curious visitors marveled at exotic displays of birds, animals, and the first dinosaurs ever discovered.

At home, Teedie practiced stuffing and mounting birds he shot for his own little museum in the back hallway. It took patience, good instruments, and a number of toxic chemicals including arsenic and formaldehyde. But with time, Teedie became an accomplished taxidermist.

In the winter of 1870–71, the Roosevelts again ventured across the Atlantic to the warm climate of the Mediterranean. This time, Teedie adored their trip. The family visited Egypt and sailed up the Nile River. They moved on to the Holy Land, which Teedie had read about in the Bible, as well as Syria, Greece, and Turkey in the Ottoman Empire.

In Egypt, Teedie put his taxidermy skills to good work. His father gave him a new gun for Christmas, and Teedie shot birds and prepared them to take home. Teedie had

read enough to appreciate his visits to Egyptian temples and holy places in Palestine, but collecting birds highlighted his trip. Oddly enough, he often looked like a stork himself. Teedie liked to read standing up, balancing on one leg with the other crossed over.

Some of the Roosevelt clan posed for this picture in Germany in 1873. They are (left to right) Theodore Roosevelt, Elliott Roosevelt, cousin Maud Elliott, Corinne Roosevelt, and cousin John Elliott.

Teedie Roosevelt stuffed and mounted (from left to right) a spur-winged lapwing, Egyptian plover, and white-tailed lapwing. Years later he gave them to the American Museum of Natural History.

Theodore Roosevelt Collection, Harvard University Library

Working Out

Young Teedie's parents continued to take the family to the country each summer in hopes that the fresh air would relieve their son's asthma attacks. But a cure never came.

When Teedie was about 13, his parents packed him off by himself on a trip to Maine. On the coach ride north, Teedie's life changed. Other boys rode along, and in Teedie—skinny, weak, nearsighted, and asthmatic—they found their mark. They picked at him and bullied him until finally he struck out in anger. The boys simply jeered and "handled me with easy contempt," as he recalled.

Teedie had never felt so humiliated. He decided to make a change. He consulted his father, who had urged his son to build his body. Now Theodore Roosevelt Sr. hired a prizefighter to teach Teedie to box.

"I felt a great admiration for men who could hold their own in the world," he wrote. His father, his Bulloch uncles, and characters in the sagas he read—all were heroes in Teedie's eyes. Determined to be helpless no longer, Teedie set out to make his body as strong as his mind. He spent long hours lifting weights and doing pull-ups on bars on an upstairs porch. Neighbors feared he would lose his balance and fall off.

He knew he would never be a champion, but in time, Teedie took pride in his strength. He grew to manhood relishing all kinds of physical activity. He learned to sit a horse well, to scramble over fences, to row, and to bike. If there were a river to swim, he would swim it. A mountain to climb, he was there. A lion to face, he would face it.

Teedie Roosevelt could not be a prize fighter, but he prized a life of vigor and action, what he famously called "the strenuous life."

BUILD YOUR BODY

TEEDIE ROOSEVELT found fun in brisk walks, rowing boats, playing tennis, and general horsing around. As a man, Theodore Roosevelt said often that a fit body must accompany a sound mind.

How fit are you? Do you enjoy exercise and sports, or are you a couch potato? Here's a test to help compare your fitness with other boys and girls your age.

NOTE: These activities appear in a handbook titled *Get Fit and Be Active!* published by the President's Council on Physical Fitness. Download it at www.presidentschallenge.org/pdf/getfit.pdf. The Council offers an Active Lifestyle Award. First, you pledge to be active for 60 minutes each day at least five days a week. Then, for a period of six weeks, you keep a log to track your results. Check out the Web site at www.presidentschallenge.org. Then click on "Kids" on the left to get started.

What's "active"? Anything from raking leaves to shooting hoops to taking a dance class—it's *moving* that counts. Kids ages 6 to 17 need to be active 60 minutes a day. Or, if you have a pedometer, you can count steps instead. Girls need to take at least 11,000 steps each day, and boys need 13,000.

Still not sure what you want to do? Take a look at these possible activities. Then get out there and move.

HOW FIT ARE YOU?

Activity	Count	What Kids Ages 9-12 Can Do	Your Score
Curl-ups	How many in one minute?	GIRLS: 30-35; BOYS: 32-40	_____
1-Mile Run/Walk	What was your time?	GIRLS: 11.3-12.5 min. BOYS: 10.6-11.9 min.	_____
Pull-ups	How many in one minute?	GIRLS: 1; BOYS: 2	_____
V-Sit Reach	How far did you reach?	GIRLS: 2.0-3.5 inches BOYS: 0.5-3.0 inches	_____
Shuttle Run (lines 30 feet apart)	What was your time?	GIRLS: 11.3-12.5 seconds BOYS: 10.6-11.9 seconds	_____

aerobics
archery
badminton
backpacking
baseball
basketball
baton twirling
bicycling
bowling
boxing
calisthenics
canoeing
cardio machines
cheerleading
children's games
cross-country skiing
curling
dancing
diving

downhill skiing
fencing
field hockey
football
Frisbee
gardening
golf
gymnastics
handball
hiking
hockey
home repair
horseback riding
horseshoe pitching
household tasks
hunting
interactive video
    sports
juggling

kayaking
kickboxing
lacrosse
lawn mowing
lifting/hauling
marching
martial arts
mountain biking
mountain climbing
Nordic walking
orienteering
paddleball
pedometer
pilates
racquetball
rock climbing
rope jumping
rowing
rugby

running
sailing
scuba diving
shuffleboard
skateboarding
skating
ski jumping
sledding
snorkeling
snowboarding
snowshoeing
snow shoveling
soccer
softball
squash
stationary bike
stretching
surfing
swimming

table tennis
tai chi
tennis
track and field
trampoline
unicycling
volleyball
walking
wallyball
water aerobics
water polo
waterskiing
weight training
whitewater rafting
windsurfing
wrestling
yoga

2

Theodore

As soon as Teedie returned from adventures in Europe, he faced an assignment. Just three years ahead loomed the prospect of entering Harvard College, but he was in no way ready. He had never gone to school.

Teedie's tutors, travels, and huge appetite for books grounded him well in the classics, nature, French, and German. However, his numbers skills needed work. His father hired a private tutor, and Teedie spent his days working on mathematics and Latin. In two years he crammed in the work of three and passed Harvard's entrance exam. He became the first of a long line of Roosevelts to enter the nation's oldest college in Cambridge, Massachusetts.

A Harvard Man

No longer the child dubbed Teedie but a college student calling himself Theodore, the young man moved into a boarding house on Winthrop Street near Harvard Square. His family felt that a damp dormitory would endanger his health. Theodore was free to furnish his room exactly as he wished. He hung animal heads on the walls and brought along snakes, lobsters, and a huge turtle.

Theodore planned to study natural science at Harvard but soon found that meant spending too much time indoors peering into a microscope. Besides, he soon became far too busy with campus life to sit still. He debated everyone—students and professors alike. He went to dances and wrote letters home about the girls he met. He marched in political parades, rowed on the Charles River, and boxed his way past many a bloody nose.

Theodore accepted invitations to join Harvard's elite social clubs. He cultivated the accent of young Boston-bred men who dropped the "r" when they said "Hah-vud." He continued his plan of bodybuilding, and when he felt that his legs were still too skinny, Theodore started jumping rope on his front porch.

Only one thing marred his happiness. When Theodore came home for Christmas during his sophomore year, he found his father gravely ill. But then, with his "Teedie" at home, his father rallied as Christmas came and went. Relieved, Theodore returned to school to study for exams.

Then his father sickened once more, but the family kept the news hidden as Theodore studied. All through January and into February, Theodore's father lay dying. Then, just at the end, Theodore received a telegram ordering him home.

His heart filled with dread, Theodore jumped on a night boat from Boston to New

Harvard student Theodore Roosevelt wears a sculling outfit for rowing on the river. Theodore Roosevelt Collection, Harvard University Library

York. He arrived at the steps of the family brownstone, only to see that a crowd had gathered. His father had died during the night.

As the winter dragged on, Theodore grew depressed. He wrote about his father in his diary, but he refused to show his dark mood to others. Thus began a pattern that he carried through life. He resolved to bury his sadness, to soldier on by working both his mind and body.

When summer came, the Roosevelts, wearing the black of mourning, left New York for Oyster Bay. There, Theodore continued his quiet grief. He didn't talk about it, but his despair showed as he began to act out of character. He rode his horse too hard. When a neighbor dog kept chasing his horse, he shot it.

Theodore still liked to keep company with Edith Carow on summer outings. But then something happened. Theodore and Edith, friends since they were small, stopped speaking without telling anyone why. Theodore left Oyster Bay to spend the rest of his summer in the Maine woods.

His days tramping about lifted Theodore's spirits. In the wilderness, the sad young man made a new friend in Bill Sewell, a tough outdoorsman who served as Theodore's guide. The rich Harvard student and the plain-speaking

Sewell clicked. "We hitched up well somehow or other from the start," Sewell said.

He was fair minded, Theodore was. And then he took pains to learn everything. There was nothing beneath his notice. I liked him right off. I liked him clear through. There wasn't a quality in him I didn't like. He wasn't headlong or aggressive, except when necessary, and as far as I could see he wasn't a bit cocky, though other folks thought so.

Then Sewell added, "I will say he wasn't remarkably cautious about expressing his opinion."

Falling in Love

As BILL Sewell noticed, Theodore liked to say what he thought. In a day when Harvard men tried to act quiet and cool, Theodore Roosevelt was neither. His classmates noticed his frankness, his enthusiasm, and his honesty. Everywhere he went, the student with the dark blond hair, red sideburns, big teeth, and spectacles could be counted on to make an entrance.

At Harvard, Theodore discovered the world was his stage, and he loved to play to the crowd. His high-pitched outbursts of joy and approval—"Bully!" and "Dee-lighted!"—became the trademark phrases he carried through life.

Theodore especially hoped to capture the fancy of Alice Hathaway Lee of Chestnut Hill, whom he met through Harvard friends. Tall and blond, Alice's sweet temperament charmed Theodore. "See that girl?" he said to a chum. "She won't have me, but I am going to have *her*!"

Theodore's hobby of collecting birds, fish, and insects did not sweep Alice off her feet. Their courtship proved to be a rocky path for Theodore. Sometimes he fell into depression when he thought he could not win her. He called on Alice constantly. When they were apart, he wrote her long letters. He trained his riding horse to pull a fancy "trap"—a tall carriage with a seat for two—and drove it to Alice's home to take her out. Rumors spread that Theodore even imported a pair of French pistols in case he would ever have to meet a rival in a duel. (The pistols stayed in their box, unused.)

In time, Theodore's charm and "bully" personality won Alice. They became engaged during Theodore's senior year, as his Harvard career came to its climax. Theodore had dealt with his father's death, and now he seized the day to make the most of Harvard.

"De-lighted!" reads a leather postcard showing Theodore Roosevelt as a cowman.

He took part in everything he could, including teaching Sunday school. Whether in art, politics, theater, debate, economics, wrestling, or boxing, Theodore Roosevelt had an interest—and an opinion.

When he graduated in June 1880, he was 21st in his class of 160 men and was a member of Phi Beta Kappa, the nation's top college honor.

That October, Theodore and Alice Lee married and moved in with Mittie in New York. Alice joined Mittie and Theodore's sisters in the round of social calls, charity events, dinner parties, and balls that marked their lives.

Theodore, meanwhile, was in his first year of law school at Columbia University and "reading law" in his uncle's firm. He had free time, however, to work on a pet project. During his Harvard years, he had wanted to read about the American navy during the War of 1812. When he could not find a book about the subject, he started to write one.

The battles, frigates, and sloops of the U.S. Navy and Great Britain's Royal Navy fascinated Theodore. He discovered that the U.S. Navy did a poor job of defending America's shores in 1812. Theodore placed the blame

Alice Hathaway Lee.
Theodore Roosevelt Collection, Harvard University Library

directly on Presidents Thomas Jefferson and James Madison for not building a strong navy. The young historian drew a lesson from his research: he believed that the U.S. Navy of the 1880s stood in equally bad shape.

The next summer, Alice Lee and Theodore took a trip through Europe. Happy and deeply in love, the young groom showed his bride the sights. They sailed down the Rhine, rode gondolas in Venice, shopped in Paris, and visited the tomb of Napoleon, the Frenchman who had conquered so much of Europe only years before. When they visited Switzerland, Theodore left Alice long enough to climb the Matterhorn, Europe's famous mountain peak. Theodore also wrote more chapters for his book on navy history. He was living as never before.

The time away from law school and home helped Theodore reflect on what he wanted from life. He decided to move in a new direction.

"Mr. Speaker!"

THE YOUNG couple returned home from Europe to a changing city. New York was home to people of huge wealth and extreme poverty.

Wealthy New Yorkers enjoyed life in the nation's Gilded Age. Newly rich captains of industry named Vanderbilt and Rockefeller

SAIL AWAY

WHEN THEODORE Roosevelt was a boy, children enjoyed sailing model boats on Central Park Lake in New York City. Often these boats were miniature works of art carved from wood and powered by handkerchief sails.

You can enjoy a 21st-century sailing experience with a twist: build a model sailboat out of recycled materials. Study this photo for hints on how sailboats are constructed, and then build your own out of things you find at home.

Library of Congress LC-USZ62-70066

Use materials that are headed for your trash, such as foam packing inserts or plastic containers. Craft materials such as balsa wood also will work.

Adult supervision required

You'll Need
❖ Piece of Styrofoam, approximately 6" x 9"
❖ Pencil
❖ Ruler
❖ Knife with a serrated (jagged) edge
❖ Cutting board
❖ Thick nail or knitting needle
❖ 1 large (milk shake–sized) drinking straw, about 8 inches long
❖ White craft glue
❖ Scissors
❖ Duct tape
❖ 3 narrow drinking straws (that will fit inside the large straw), about 8 inches long
❖ Heavy plastic bag
❖ Sinkful of water
❖ Several washers or quarters

1. Take the material you have chosen for your boat's hull (the frame, or body, of the boat), most likely a piece of recycled Styrofoam. You can look for one that is already shaped like a boat, or use the pencil and ruler to draw an outline on the foam.

Think: how are boats shaped? Yours will sail better if you draw a point at one end to create a bow, the forward part of the boat. With an adult to help you, use the knife to cut out your boat on the cutting board.

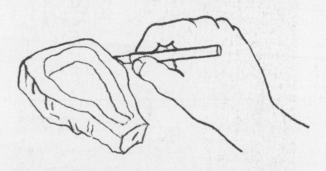

2. Use a nail to make a small hole in the center bottom of your boat. Don't poke it all the way through. Cut a 2½-inch piece from the big straw.

continued . . .

Cut one end into a point and insert it in the center of your boat to make the mast holder. Pour glue all around the straw so that it flows down the hole and puddles around the straw. Set aside to dry completely.

3. Before you begin, cut several strips of duct tape about ½ inch wide and set them aside. To make the sail and mast that will fit into the mast holder, join the three narrow drinking straws end to end by squishing 1 inch of one end and inserting it into the next one. Look at the diagram and fold the straws into the shape of the numeral "4." Secure the corners with tiny pieces of duct tape,

then use more tape to fasten the straws to the mast. The triangle part of the "4" will serve as the edge of your sail.

4. To make a sail, cut a piece of thin plastic slightly larger than the straw triangle and lay it down on a flat surface. Now run a heavy line of glue along the edge of the straw triangle only. Place it on top of the plastic and tap it gently down to secure. Set it aside to dry thoroughly.

5. When the sail is dry, trim the excess plastic away from its edges. Insert the "leg" of the "4"

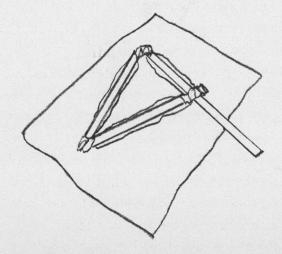

into the straw mast holder in the bottom of your boat. The sail should move freely so it will "catch" the wind.

6. Fill a sink or bathtub with water. Does your boat float well? If it's top-heavy, you might need to add ballast—something to stabilize it—by inserting washers or quarters into the bottom of the hull.

7. It's time to try out your masterpiece outside. Be sure an adult is along if you decide to sail your boat in a lake or pond.

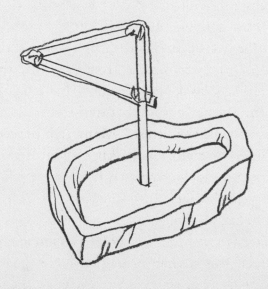

constructed huge mansions on Fifth Avenue that outdid the brownstones of the Roosevelts and other old-money families. A list titled "Four Hundred" was printed in the city's social register. These people of means ran New York's businesses, private clubs, museums, opera, and charities. But a bursting middle class demanded its share of the good life as well. Its children went to school, and a lucky few went on to high school.

At the bottom rung of the social ladder stood the city's immigrants, who squeezed their families into shabby tenements in slums. People of the lower classes worked from Monday through Saturday, often ten or more hours a day. Their children also worked at jobs and got little schooling.

When the upper classes thought about poor people, many took a cue from Charles Darwin, whose book about evolution had created a stir. Darwin wrote that nature demands "survival of the fittest." Many rich people thought Darwin was talking about *them*. After all, they had survived and made it to the top of society. Such thinking was called social Darwinism.

Darwin never meant for his ideas to apply to men and women in human society. But social Darwinism twisted Darwin's theories to try to explain why rich people were successful. They were the "fittest." Social Darwinists said that poor people had only themselves to blame. If an individual was to have a better life, he or she must work for it.

Theodore Roosevelt grew to manhood believing in personal responsibility as well. But neither Roosevelt nor his father was a social Darwinist. Roosevelt's father, who lived in a high-minded way, worked hard at his job and did good works to help the poor. Theodore the father had performed his good works as a private citizen. Theodore the son decided that *he* would do good works in public office.

Young Roosevelt started to dip his toes into politics. Wealthy men did not hold public office in the 1880s. Friends warned Roosevelt that politics was "low," that he would have to hang out with "saloon keepers, horse-car conductors, and the like."

Machine politics ruled the day across the United States, when a handful of bosses ruled both Democrats and Republicans. As states and cities grew, so did their political machines. Greedy politicians handed out spoils—dollars that made sure they won and held power. New York City laid in control of Tammany Hall, the nickname for the Democrats and their party bosses who ran New York politics like a well-oiled engine.

Roosevelt joined the Republican Party, a Lincoln Republican like his father, who had

This photo of Theodore Roosevelt was taken in 1886, when he was 28 years old. Sagamore Hill National Historic Site

stood for the Union in the Civil War. However, just becoming a member of the party meant little. Like anyone else who wanted a job in government, Roosevelt would have to pay his dues to Republicans in his home district.

Party regulars met in a room over a bar that smelled of smoke and stale beer. These rough-and-tumble men were not the same kind of Republicans as those in Theodore's social circle. When Theodore walked through the door looking to join their club, they rolled their eyes. However, one of the regulars, a rough man named Joe Murray, looked past the trappings of wealth and the Harvard accent that clung to Roosevelt like jewels in a crown.

He liked Roosevelt's bold, brash ways and began to coach him in street politics. There were bumps at first, but within months Roosevelt won the party's nomination for a seat in the New York State Assembly. In the 21st District, solidly Republican, a nomination was as good as the final vote.

Murray shepherded Roosevelt through the general election in the fall of 1882. Roosevelt had to win backing from working men who hung out in taverns, as well as gentlemen who enjoyed brandy and cigars in the smoking rooms of mansions. Murray taught his outspoken pupil to hold back on some opinions. Politics, Roosevelt discovered, took both strong views and a delicate touch. He won the election.

All flash and vigor, Roosevelt arrived in Albany, New York's state capital, on January 2, 1882. As usual, his teeth, glasses, and loud voice heralded his arrival. He was quite the "dude," well-dressed for his new role.

Both sides made fun as Roosevelt leaned out from his seat like an eager schoolboy, yelling, "Mr. Speaker! Mr. Speaker!" Yet Roosevelt declared he "rose as fast as a rocket" in New York politics. He thought that most of his fellow assemblymen were either corrupt or incompetent, unable to do anything. Like it or not, politics was a game of power—a game to be played. Sometimes the players cheated, lied, stole, or changed sides to get what they wanted.

Seeking Balance

WHEN ROOSEVELT left for Albany, he shared other Republicans' views about a person's property. Businessmen, he felt, had the right to use their land and buildings as they wished. Government should not tell a man how to run his business. But in Albany, Roosevelt met Samuel Gompers, an immigrant and union leader. Gompers worked to improve the lives of families who made cigars in their tenement homes. Cigar makers were using their employees' homes as factories, and Gompers wanted the New York Assembly to outlaw the practice. Roosevelt, along with other Republicans, fought the idea. Roosevelt felt that a man should use his property as he wished.

Then Gompers asked Roosevelt to tour the tenements. Roosevelt could not believe what he saw: fathers, mothers, and children crowded into tiny apartments, rolling cigars alongside "foul bedding" and "scraps of food." He had never seen such human misery. From then on, Roosevelt backed Gompers's efforts, although years passed before the Assembly changed the law.

Over the years, Roosevelt grew to prize fairness, especially between business owners

Boys at work in a cigar factory posed for this 1909 photo. Library of Congress LC-DIG-nclc-04506

Alice Roosevelt Longworth

President Theodore Roosevelt once admitted that he could either run the country or control his daughter Alice—he "could not possibly do both." Through her long life, she made a name for herself.

However, Alice's name was never spoken at home. When her mother Alice Lee died, Theodore locked up memories of his beloved wife. He never spoke her name again. Nor could he bring himself to call his daughter by her name. Among the Roosevelts, Alice was simply "Sister" or "Sis." Decades later, Alice's great nieces and nephews called her "Aunt Sister."

Theodore's second wife, Edith Roosevelt, raised Alice as her own child, but from a young age Alice seemed to feel different. Only her Aunt Bamie spoke about her dead mother.

Alice Roosevelt Longworth
Library of Congress LC-USZ62-83139

Theodore never did. Alice dealt with this gap in her life by breaking every rule she could.

Pretty and bright, Alice had a wild streak and could be bratty. She smoked in public, a horror among proper ladies. She carried a small green snake in her purse—named Emily Spinach after Edith's skinny sister. Popular with the press, she dressed in a distinctive color that newspapers called "Alice blue."

Alice had her own money she received from her Lee grandparents. To Theodore's dismay, she ran with a rich, spoiled crowd. Then a congressman named Nicholas Longworth, who was 14 years older, caught her eye. Their White House wedding in 1906 was the talk of the nation.

The marriage had problems. Nick had an eye for the ladies, and Alice turned to others for the affection she craved. She had a baby girl, Paulina, who almost certainly was the child of a U.S. senator. Paulina had a troubled life and died young. Alice raised her granddaughter, Joanna Sturm. The old woman and young girl grew close.

Alice's tart tongue and sharp opinions made her a media favorite for decades. Often she appeared on the White House guest list. She died at the age of 96 in 1980.

and people who worked for them. Like the members of his social class, he valued individual achievement. He felt that each person is in charge of making life a success. Unlike many others, however, Roosevelt decided that his duty stretched beyond personal to "collective responsibility." He feared that a group of greedy, lawless businessmen would destroy civilization. He asked himself, how can I work in government to make things fair for everyone?

Roosevelt could dream about fairness, but he needed to be realistic. He had to use the art of give-and-take. In order to succeed as a leader he must ask, how can I keep one side in balance against the other?

Fairness and balance became double themes in Theodore Roosevelt's political life.

"The Light of My Life"

Busy as he was learning the ropes in the New York Assembly, Theodore Roosevelt spent every moment he could enjoying life. In the summer of 1882, he joined Elliott for a hunting trip in Iowa and Minnesota. Back in New York City, he and Alice Lee shared a new home on West 45th Street. When they visited the countryside of Oyster Bay, Theodore joyfully bought property on a hilltop overlooking Long Island Sound. Buildings began to rise on the sprawling estate. Theodore named it Leeholm for Alice's family.

By the next summer of 1883, Alice and Theodore looked forward to the first baby for Leeholm's nursery. Alice stayed busy preparing for the new arrival surrounded by Theodore's mother and sisters. Theodore, on break from the Assembly, returned west.

Early in September 1883 he ventured farther in search of buffalo in the Dakota Territory. His destination was a windswept place called the Badlands, where erosion from air and water had carved out a strange, haunted landscape. Despite the dangers of hunting, Theodore thrived. He bought property called the Maltese Cross Ranch. He wrote Alice that he would "bring you home the head of a great buffalo bull."

For eight days my bad luck was steady. On the ninth it culminated . . . we found the very fresh track of a large buffalo bull . . . when I caught sight of him feeding at the bottom of a steep gulley: I crawled up to the edge, not thirty yards from great, grim looking beast, and sent a shot from the heavy rifle into him just behind his shoulder, the ball going clean through his body. He dropped dead before going a hundred yards.

Back home, in November 1883, Theodore easily won a third term in the State Assembly and returned to Albany. Alice moved in with Mittie in Theodore's old family home. The new baby was due in mid-February, and Theodore waited for the telegram to call him home.

On February 11, 1884, the telegram arrived. Alice had given birth to a baby girl. As Theodore received handshakes from other lawmakers, another telegram arrived. Alice was gravely ill.

Theodore caught the next train south and rushed to his mother's home. At midnight he

Theodore Roosevelt (left) and his brother Elliott enjoyed their hunting trips in America's West.
Sagamore Hill National Historic Site, National Park Service

MAP ROOSEVELT'S TRAVELS, AND YOURS

BY THE time he entered Harvard, Theodore Roosevelt had sailed twice to Europe and the Middle East.

Where have you traveled with your family?

You can compare your journeys with Roosevelt's easily on a world map. Or if your family hasn't ventured beyond the United States, you may choose to plot your journeys on a U.S. map.

You'll Need

❖ Maps of Europe and the Middle East for Theodore's travels

❖ U.S. map or world map for your travels

❖ Glue stick or rubber cement

❖ Foam core board or bulletin board with tacks

❖ Long pins

❖ Construction paper in two colors

❖ Scissors

❖ Pen or marker

❖ Piece of paper

Print out the PDF versions of maps of Europe, the Middle East, and the United States from this Central Intelligence Agency Web site: https://www.cia.gov/library/publications/the-world-factbook (click on "Regional Maps").

Glue the maps to the foam core board or tack them to a bulletin board. The maps of Europe and the Middle East should go next to each other. Your map, either the U.S. map or world map, goes below.

Label the maps as shown below.

Cut small triangles from one color of construction paper. Using chapters 1 and 2 as a guide, list the cities that Teedie Roosevelt visited with his family when he was a child. Mark each triangle with the name of each.

Thread each triangle onto a long pin to make a flag. Find its location on the map of Europe or Middle East and stick it with the pin.

Now it's *your* turn. Choose the map of the United States, the world map, or both. List all the cities, states, and countries you have visited. Use the second color of paper to make a set of flags.

Then, pinpoint all the places you've seen on your map.

Do any of your destinations match up with Roosevelt's?

Think: as you read more about Roosevelt's life in this book, will you be able to match up his travels with places you have seen?

burst through the door and got the horrible news. Alice was dying of kidney failure, and his mother was deathly sick with typhoid fever. Mittie died at three o'clock in the morning on February 14. Upstairs, Alice was slipping away. At two o'clock that afternoon, as Theodore held her in his arms, she died. Alice's pregnancy had hidden her kidney disease from her doctor. She was just 22.

Two days later, Theodore sat frozen with shock through a double funeral at the Fifth Avenue Presbyterian Church. Family and friends, including Edith Carow, surrounded him. Alice and Mittie were buried next to one another as the young widower looked down into their graves.

Soon thereafter, Theodore and his family returned to the church as his new daughter was baptized. He named her Alice Lee for her mother.

Theodore believed that his life was lived out at age 25. Never could he love another woman with the fire of his love for Alice. It seemed that Theodore Roosevelt locked up his heart and threw away the key. When he wrote his autobiography years later, he never wrote about Alice.

Theodore's older sister Bamie agreed to care for Baby Lee, as the family called Theo-

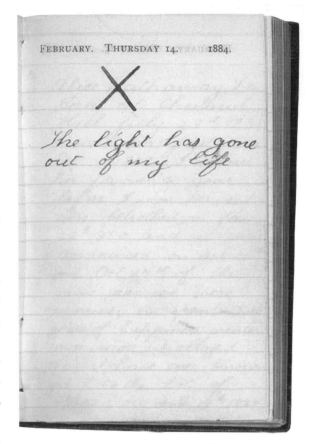

Theodore Roosevelt's diary entry spoke for itself on February 14, 1882. The next entry, which he wrote in memory of his dead wife, shows through the paper.
Library of Congress

dore's little girl. Then he returned to Albany to complete his term in the General Assembly. It was time for Theodore Roosevelt to go back to work.

3

Mr. Roosevelt, Ranchman

IN JUNE 1884, Roosevelt boarded a train for Chicago to serve as a delegate to the Republican Convention.

Roosevelt kept his grief bottled up as he took his first steps onto the national stage. But he was willing to show his heart for reform. As loud as ever, he spoke out against the Republican candidate, James G. Blaine. Blaine's record, littered with charges of dirty deals, offended Roosevelt. He and others who backed reform candidates became known as mugwumps.

Blaine was popular. Backers called him the Plumed Knight and managed to nominate Blaine for president. In the end, Roosevelt felt it was his duty to back him in the November election. However, voters looking for change sent Grover Cleveland, a Democrat, to Washington.

Brash and bold, Theodore Roosevelt made a name for himself among both Republicans and Democrats during 1884. He was just 25 years old. True, he made enemies, but he also drew important people to his side. As he worked all night at meetings and spent all day on the convention floor, Roosevelt forged a close friendship with a Bostonian named Henry Cabot Lodge. Lodge, also from a prominent family, had the same zeal for reform. Ten years older than Roosevelt, he was a quieter, courtly man. Although the two quarreled over politics later in life, their friendship endured. They sent letters back and forth for 25 years that eventually filled two thick books.

Despite Theodore Roosevelt's grand entrance into national politics, his life lay in tatters. On the outside, he politicked with a bully look. On the inside, he nursed a broken heart, and he decided to leave his seat in the New York General Assembly. Instead, he would go far from home, thousands of miles from the sights and sounds that reminded him of Alice.

Theodore boarded the train for Chicago, where he switched to a line on the Northern Pacific Railway. His destination was a small town in the Badlands of Dakota.

Good Months in the Badlands

THE DUSTY, dry twin towns of Little Missouri and Medora that sat on either side of the Little Missouri River were not much to see. But to the pale, heartsick Roosevelt, who was recovering from another bout of the stomach trouble that bothered him from time to time, their few wooden buildings and colorful citizens promised a new way of life.

Here in the Badlands, in the heart of the Dakota Territory, times were changing. Well-heeled young men arrived to make fortunes by raising cattle. There were Americans, Britons, and a glamorous French nobleman named the Marquis de Mores who lived in a grand wooden chateau (mansion) and planned to build a cattle empire. With an initial investment of $14,000, Roosevelt joined them.

He had a lot to learn. The fancy-looking "dude" who came on the train packed a Winchester rifle with sterling silver trim and a hunting knife from Tiffany's jewelers in New York. Folks poked fun at his gun and knife

PLAY IN THE DIRT TO STOP EROSION

CHILDREN IN Theodore Roosevelt's day made their own fun. Sometimes boys and girls created miniature worlds out of soil, rocks, twigs, and pinecones. They staged their own dramas on these tiny landscapes. With a watering can, they could even cause storms and floods. Erosion wiped out their small creations—just as it swept soil into America's streams and rivers.

You can play in the dirt and become a soil scientist, too. Discover how erosion works by building a landscape and making "rain." Use your imagination—can you build a landscape to defy erosion?

You'll Need

❖ Bare spot of earth outside where you can dig
❖ Trowel or large, old spoon
❖ Natural material—rocks, sticks, leaves, grass, moss, shells, and small branches
❖ Toy trucks, cars, houses, or action figures
❖ Watering can

Before you start, check with an adult that you are digging in a safe place. Then plan out a landscape. Let your imagination run wild. Pile up dirt into mountains and carve valleys between them. Dig out lakes and rivers. Be sure that at least one of your hills stands at least eight inches tall. Use natural materials to add features to your landscape. Then populate your creation with small action figures and toys.

Now make it rain using a watering can or sprinkler bottle. How do the landforms you built and the natural features you added affect the amount of erosion on your hill? Think: is there a way to build the hill to slow down erosion? (In the 1930s, a farmer discovered contour farming and planted rows of crops to follow the curve of hills to prevent erosion.)

Have fun playing in the dirt. Now you are a soil scientist!

Erosion from wind and rain carved out the Badlands.
National Park Service Digital Image Archives

and wondered how a young fool like this one could survive in the raw land they called home.

But once Roosevelt shed his traveling outfit and put on his buckskins, a new ranchman emerged. Roosevelt could breathe in the freedom that the West promised. His eyes drank in the vast grasslands, big sky, and cascades of color that swept across the Badlands at dawn and dusk.

It was rough country, with rattlesnakes the size of his arm and quicksand that could suck in a man and his horse without warning. A vein of coal ran just underground. At spots where it poked out, it seemed the land caught fire and smoldered with acrid fumes.

To the men who ran cattle in the Badlands, it was open land ripe for fattening cows before they were rounded up and shipped to market. Only a few trappers lived there. Native people were gone, forced out during the Indian Wars of the 1870s and '80s. The U.S. government pushed the Lakota (Sioux) onto reservations in far-flung places, and they lost their freedom to roam the Badlands. With fresh memories of mass murder on both sides, there was no trust between "red men" and "white men."

Early on, Roosevelt came across a party of Indians on horseback. He did not hesitate to dismount his horse, face them, and point his rifle to show his strength. In turn, they followed him for miles until they finally rode off. To Roosevelt, the threat was real; the sorry fact was that whites killed Indians, and Indians killed whites.

A friend wrote later that:

Roosevelt on one occasion recovered two horses which had been stolen from an old Indian. The Indian took them, muttering something that sounded like "Um, um," and without a word or a gesture of gratitude rode away with his property. Roosevelt felt cheap, as though he had done a service which had not been appreciated; but a few days later the old Indian came to him and silently laid in his arms a hide bearing an elaborate painting of the battle of the Little Big Horn.

Theodore Roosevelt and Native Americans

In a day when most whites thought of Indians as savages or childlike at best, Roosevelt stood apart. He could make outrageous statements about people in general, and as a young man he made some about Indians. Still, other Lakota saw that Roosevelt's view differed from most. He was his father's son, and he judged each person as a man or woman. Indians, he felt, had rights just as whites did.

When Roosevelt became president, he relied on the advice of men who worked closely with native people. As always, Roosevelt wanted everyone—American Indians included—to have an opportunity to work hard and make a better life.

Can You Hear the Buzz?

ALL ACROSS the Americas, native children played with toy buzzers, spinning disks that made a soothing sound. Such toys were made of bone or antler. Pioneer children learned to make similar buzzers from buttons or disks of wood.

You'll Need

- ❖ Ruler
- ❖ Thin piece of nylon string or fishing line
- ❖ Scissors
- ❖ Large, flat, round button—not too thick, and at least 1 inch wide

Cut a piece of nylon string 25 inches long. Thread one end of the string through one hole in the button. Then thread it back through the hole opposite the first.

Using a square knot (instructions below), tie the ends of the string to make a loop.

Center your buzzer in the middle of the string loop. Slip your index fingers into each end and twirl the buzzer so that the string "winds up." Done properly, your hands will move closer together.

Gently pull your hands apart so that the string unwinds, and then allow the string to rewind and pull your hands back together. Repeat this process in a gentle, continuous motion.

Do you hear the buzz?

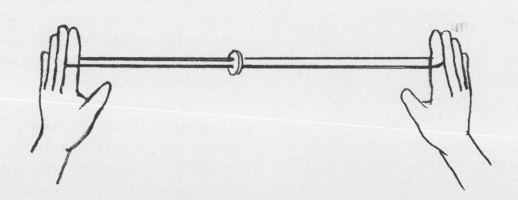

To Make a Square Knot

Tying a square knot is like tying your shoe, except that you tie twice.

First, tie a single knot going right over left, just like tying your shoe. Pull both ends a bit.

Repeat, except that this time, tie left over right.

Pull both ends tightly. You've made a square knot!

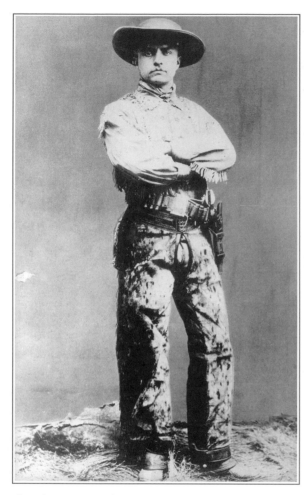

Theodore Roosevelt posed in his ranching gear for a New York photographer. Sagamore Hill National Historic Site, National Park Service

Beautiful as the painted hide was, the gift offered a message. In 1876, Lakota warriors had defeated General George Armstrong Custer, a glory-seeker who led his soldiers into battle at the Little Big Horn River. The Lakota killed every one.

A Living Legend

ROOSEVELT HIRED Bill Sewell and Will Dow, woodsmen from Maine, to come west. There in the Badlands, Roosevelt partnered with Bill Merrifield to run the Maltese Cross Ranch with Sewall and Dow as managers. Theodore Roosevelt, after all, was no mere cowboy. He was a ranchman, with hundreds of head of cattle to prove it. (After Alice died, he had bought more land, a second ranch named the Elkhorn.)

Though Roosevelt enjoyed hanging out with the cowboys who worked for him, they never doubted who was boss. Spectacles and all, he was Mr. Roosevelt. But when he joined them on the range, they nearly fell out of their saddles laughing. Their young leader urged them on in his best Harvard accent, "Hasten forward quickly there!"

But the tenderfoot proved his grit. He rode in the hot summer sun and stood guard over the herd during the cold nights of the fall roundup, just like any other cowboy. When the cattle spooked and stampeded, he chased them for miles in darkness when even his horse could not see. Another cowboy's mount was killed running into a tree in the dark.

Roosevelt's skin weathered from sun and wind. Days in the saddle toughened him like no workout in New York ever could. As a rider and marksman, he was nothing special, but the men around him discovered that he was made of exceptional stuff. He worked hard, and he never gave up. As tiring as his days could be, he wrote about his adventures at night by lantern light, later published in a book, *Hunting Trips of a Ranchman.*

Roosevelt had started out with the nickname Four-Eyes, but soon he lost it after a drunk in a bar pointed his gun and suggested that Four-Eyes buy everyone a drink. "Well if I've got to, I've got to," Roosevelt said. Then he stood up, and with a right-left-right, Four-Eyes punched the drunk out.

No one called him Teddy, as his wife Alice once had. Alice was a memory. Even when Bill Sewell, who had a little girl of his own, mentioned their daughter, Roosevelt replied that his baby Alice Lee was better off living with her aunt.

Back in New York, Roosevelt's uncles, the family members with good heads for business, fussed that all his notions about ranching were bad ones. How would cattle survive the bitter Dakota winters, when temperatures dropped so far below zero the thermometers actually froze?

But during that first winter, Roosevelt's cattle did well. As spring 1885 came to the Badlands, ranching looked promising. Eager to succeed, Roosevelt staked about half his wealth into running cattle. All spring and summer, he continued to grow as a ranchman. He helped to form a stockmen's group in Medora and became one of its leaders.

Early the next spring, Roosevelt amazed a doctor miles off when he limped into Dickinson, North Dakota. A wagonload of thieves had stolen a boat, and Roosevelt, Sewell, and Dow had tracked them down the Little Missouri River, still running with ice. Under the laws of the territory, they had every right to hang the thieves when they captured them. But Sewell and Dow went on downriver. Roosevelt hired a wagon and driver to take the thieves by land to a sheriff in Dickinson. He walked behind them during the three-day trek, rifle in his hand, never daring to go to sleep. By the time he reached Dickinson, he needed the doctor to plaster blisters on his feet, a hot bath, and some well-deserved rest.

Theodore Roosevelt's Maltese Cross Ranch cabin went on display at the Louisiana Purchase Exposition when he was president. Theodore Roosevelt Collection, Harvard University Library

Mr. Roosevelt, Writer and Policeman

4

During his two years as a cowman, Theodore Roosevelt made frequent trips home. In September 1885, Theodore Roosevelt came home to attend to Republican Party politics and visit his family. The wind-burned man who swung down from the railway coach seemed different—but for his flashing grin, square white teeth, and telltale spectacles.

At five feet, eight inches tall, Theodore weighed thirty pounds more than when he became a ranchman. He had left a slender, brokenhearted widower, but he came back with the air of a confident, hardened man.

Edith

Everyone noticed that Theodore kept away from Edith Carow, his childhood friend. She seemed just as careful to avoid him, which took planning because she spent so much time with his sister Corinne. Though they ran in the same social circle, Theodore and Edith did not cross paths for a year and a half.

Yet despite the effort they made to stay apart, fate had its way. Theodore stopped by to visit Corinne at home. As he crossed into the front hallway, bound for the staircase leading up to the parlor, a young woman came down the steps.

It was Edith. Neither one had planned to meet; now they had no choice but to talk. Exactly what they said was a secret, but they began to keep company together. Theodore felt his feelings grow from friendship into love. Edith, who must have felt second-best to the dead Alice Lee, allowed herself to fall in love with him.

candidates. Roosevelt himself showed up in Baltimore on Election Day to witness the dirty dealing and filed a long report. But he never directly attacked Wanamaker, who had friends in high places including the White House.

President Harrison was not as eager for reform as Roosevelt, and Wanamaker kept his job. The president knew that Roosevelt's thundering manner made him as many enemies as friends. In turn, the young upstart dared to call the president "the little grey man in the White House."

But the winds of government changed again. "Reform!" was in the air, and the nation returned Grover Cleveland to the White House in the election of 1892. Cleveland the Democrat kept Roosevelt the Republican at his job. Roosevelt continued to bushwhack offenders of civil service reform.

A Cop in New York City

ROOSEVELT CONSIDERED another attempt at running for mayor of New York City in 1894. However, Edith hated the idea, so Theodore buried that thought. But in 1895 the new mayor of New York dangled the job of police commissioner in front of him. Within days, Roosevelt moved from Washington to an office in the police department on New York's Mulberry Street. Nights later, he put on a disguise and hit the street like a bloodhound, sniffing the air for shady people and corrupt enterprises.

Roosevelt became top dog among New York City's four police commissioners. He pushed for all kinds of changes. He tried with some success to establish a system for promoting good policemen up through the ranks.

When Roosevelt laid his eyes on the absurd variety of guns that police carried, he set rules for sidearms. From then on, New York

This cartoon poked fun at Theodore Roosevelt's plans to reform the Civil Service. The elephant, with President Benjamin Harrison riding on top, symbolizes the Republican Party.

Identify the Crook!

WHEN THEODORE Roosevelt became police commissioner in New York City, he needed to catch criminals who wore disguises. Roosevelt favored a method of identifying criminals developed by a Frenchman named Alphonse Bertillon. This French detective knew that, though criminals wore different disguises, their body measurements changed very little. Bertillon's measurements included the criminal's height, length of an ear, width of the cheeks, length of the forehead, and the width of the head. Once these measurements were in the hands of the police, it would be easy to identify a crook.

Was Bertillon correct? You can find out by measuring features on your head and face and then disguising yourself. What will you discover?

You'll Need

❖ A partner
❖ Ruler
❖ Pencil
❖ Your notebook (from page 3)
❖ Things around the house to help make disguises, such as makeup, hats, wigs, jewelry, scarves, cotton, yarn, and construction paper
❖ Digital camera
❖ A way to print pictures from your camera

To begin, make a chart of these four measurements in your notebook.

Have your partner use the ruler to measure each of these features.

Now for the fun part. Plan a disguise and put it on. You can change your face and head to re-create yourself as a movie character, someone in a book, or a creature that has never walked on Earth. Then, when you are ready, ask your partner to take a photo of you like a mug shot at a police station.

Continue to plan and put on as many disguises as you wish. Every time, ask your partner to take a picture of you in mug-shot style.

Print out the pictures so that they are as close as possible to the size of your head.

Line up the photos next to each other. Then stand back and take a good look at them. What

MY BERTILLON MEASUREMENTS

Forehead: _____

Ear length: _____

Width from temple to temple: _____
(Hold the ruler in front of your subject's face to get an approximate measurement from one side to the other.)

Width of cheeks: _____
(Use the same method as the temples.)

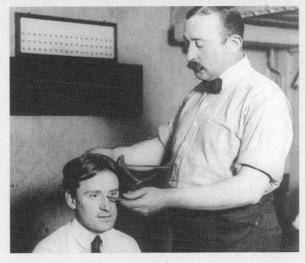

In the early 1900s, a policeman showed how to measure a man's head using the Bertillon system.
Library of Congress LC-USZ62-50068

do you notice? Use the ruler to measure your features in each mug shot.

Was Bertillon correct? If so, then each of your mug shots should have similar details that don't change very much.

Bertillon's system was quite popular for identifying criminals, but soon another, more efficient method of pinpointing crooks arose. Can you guess what it was?

Police began to use fingerprinting to identify criminals around 1900.

policemen wore six-shot, .38 caliber revolvers in their holsters. Their new boss insisted that they go to target practice.

As commissioner, Roosevelt imported a French method for identifying criminals using body measurements and photography. Roosevelt also approved as an elite squad of policemen gave "exhibitions of remarkable daring and skill" on a new, wildly popular form of transportation—bicycles.

Roosevelt at work as president of the New York City Board of Police Commissioners.
Theodore Roosevelt Collection, Harvard College Library

Within a year, Roosevelt turned the police department upside down. The public, Roosevelt knew, both accepted and expected that the police would behave like thieves. At all levels, the police were on the take, accepting bribes and looking aside when criminals broke the law—or business owners twisted it.

Every Sunday, a glaring example of graft, what newspapers called corruption, took place across New York City. The law said that beer and liquor could not be sold in public places on Sunday, neither in low-class bars nor in fine hotels. But saloonkeepers and

William Jennings Bryan, Populist and Orator

William Jennings Bryan led the Democratic Party during most of Theodore Roosevelt's political career. He ran for president three times. Bryan championed populism, a movement to make better lives for farmers and small-town Americans.

In the mid-1890s, everyday Americans faced high prices and hard times. The United States based its economy and money on one thing only: gold. The supply of money was tight, and prices were high.

Bryan based his thinking on the law of supply and demand. Silver was in great supply; Bryan believed that adding silver to the U.S. Treasury would add money to

the economy. With more money in circulation, prices would fall—as Americans' lives improved.

In 1896, Bryan ran for president against William McKinley. Bryan focused on the poor state of the economy and campaigned for the free coinage of silver.

Bryan's speech at the Democrats' convention in 1896 launched him as one of America's great speakers. He thundered, "You shall not press down on the brow of labor this crown of thorns [the gold standard], you shall not crucify mankind on a cross of gold."

William Jennings Bryan. Library of Congress LC-DIG-hec-02226

hotel owners paid the police a steady stream of cash. The police pocketed the money, and liquor flowed as easily on Sunday afternoon as on Saturday night.

Roosevelt met the problem head-on. The law was the law, he reasoned. Bribery of the police, practically in broad daylight, robbed the public of its moral spirit. So Roosevelt ordered the police to enforce the law and close down the bars on Sunday. He expected that his order would have a simple, quick result: the New York General Assembly would change the law.

But the Assembly did nothing. Many New Yorkers, especially a large group of German Americans, began to grumble. True to their culture, these working people drank the German national beverage on Sunday outings with families or friends in beer gardens. Sunday was a day to relax, the only day when men did not have to go to work.

In September, outraged German Americans organized a protest march to bring back their beloved Sunday beer. They dared Roosevelt to watch. Roosevelt showed up in good humor on the parade stand and chuckled as a coffin bearing the word "Teddyism" passed by. When one old German looked up as he marched by, he called out the commissioner. "Wo ist Roosevelt?" ("Where is Roosevelt?") Just as fast, Roosevelt leaned out and shouted back "Hier bin ich!" ("Here am I!") The German-speaking crowd loved it.

But as 1895 wore on, Roosevelt's order grew more unpopular. Newspapers began to make fun of Roosevelt's straight talk and loud manner. The Democrats from Tammany Hall crafted ways to turn New Yorkers against the Republican mayor and his wild-eyed police commissioner. Roosevelt annoyed his fellow Republicans at City Hall as well. He and another commissioner held up city business just to score points against each other.

Roosevelt had been at his police desk for a year when he started to cast about for a new job. Again, political luck eased his way. In the election of 1896 the current president, a Republican named William McKinley, fended off a challenge by the Democrat William Jennings Bryan. Roosevelt began a quiet crusade to get a job in Washington.

He started in an artful way. On a summer day, Mrs. Maria Longworth Storer, a well-off socialite and close friend of President McKinley, visited the Roosevelts at Sagamore Hill. Roosevelt, dressed in his summer best, invited the lady for a ride in his rowboat. As Roosevelt skillfully dipped his oars in Oyster Bay, he was thinking about bigger boats.

He made his case to his influential guest. "I should like," he told her, "to be assistant secretary of the navy."

An ad in 1892 showed a young woman holding a bottle of American beer labeled in German.
Library of Congress LC-DIG-ppmsca-09483

5

Colonel Roosevelt, Warrior

IN THE spring of 1897, Theodore Roosevelt switched his thinking from crime in New York to challenges on the high seas. He arrived at the Navy Department in Washington eager for excitement. He scrounged a fancy wooden desk from the basement carved with images of ships and guns and the American flag. From his chair, he could see the White House nearby.

Roosevelt was thinking about the Monroe Doctrine. In 1823 President James Monroe had stated that the United States would stop European powers that meddled in the Western Hemisphere. Since then, the United States had applied its principle: the Americas fell into its sphere of influence.

Roosevelt understood history. He knew that Americans had turned inward and did not concern themselves with world events.

In the mid-1800s there were battles enough to deal with at home. As Americans pushed westward, the U.S. Army had gone to war against Mexicans in Texas and Native Americans in Indian country.

Above all, Roosevelt understood how Americans had faced the fearsome question of holding other people as slaves. They had fought a bloody Civil War to settle that issue in 1865, but bitterness lingered.

Roosevelt saw that the world scene was shifting, too. In Europe, Germany was building a massive industry based on steel and weapons. Spain had warships stationed in its colonies in the Americas and around the globe. The United States and Great Britain, though growing closer as English-speaking democracies, still quarreled over borders between the United States and Canada.

In the Pacific, Japan's Imperial Navy boasted a shining fleet. The Russian Empire, the only nation stretching across two continents, built its navy to ensure its power on both the Atlantic and Pacific oceans.

Roosevelt believed that Americans must tackle global issues. The United States now stretched across an entire continent and held the gigantic territory of Alaska to the north. The United States had also annexed a small string of islands in the Pacific known as Hawaii. The growing nation had new interests to protect. He viewed Germany, Spain, Japan, and Russia as warlike, a threat to Americans. The answer, Roosevelt believed, was to build a stronger navy with a tough fleet of ships.

Roosevelt drew many of his plans for the navy from a book. In 1890 he had read *The Influence of Sea Power* by a British sea captain, Lord Alfred T. Mahan. Mahan advised the United States to start thinking like a world power. America, he warned, needed a strong navy to protect merchant ships as they carried U.S. goods—and to defend the United States and its territories against attack by enemy warships. The navy was building cruisers—warships to protect American merchant boats. But to Roosevelt's dismay, the navy "had no battle-ships to back them."

The navy secretary, John D. Long, followed the thinking of President McKinley. McKin-ley took little interest in foreign affairs and worried far more about America's businesses. The country was just starting to recover from a harsh depression in the mid-1890s, when one in ten Americans had no job.

Secretary Long was content to allow Roosevelt to master the details of warships and battle plans, which Roosevelt did in record time. Roosevelt practically bowled over his boss, urging the president and Congress to provide money for six new warships and scores of other vessels.

To War with Spain

To ROOSEVELT, the most serious threat to peace lay in tiny Cuba, only 90 miles from Florida's southern tip. For 30 years, the Cuban people had been in revolt against Spain, which held Cuba as a colony. Spanish soldiers were rounding up Cuban families and forcing them to live like animals in concentration camps. Roosevelt saw trouble ahead for the United States.

Newspaper publishers, including William Randolph Hearst and Joseph Pulitzer, printed shocking stories. Graphic tales of Spain's brutal behavior against defenseless Cubans appeared in the *New York Journal* and the *New York World*. Some people lashed out at Hearst and Pulitzer, calling them yellow journalists, or reporters who stretched the facts. But many Americans adored these sensationalist papers and bought tons of them.

Americans disagreed about going to war against Spain. Isolationists, including President McKinley and William Jennings Bryan, argued that the United States should stay out of other countries' problems and not take part in wars to build empires. Others, termed imperialists, who had plans to establish the United States as an empire equal to any other, made their case. War against Spain, they declared, would mean freedom for the Cuban people. Businesspeople also joined the call to arms. They counted on a steady supply of sugar cane and tobacco from Cuba for refineries and cigar makers.

In February 1898 the battleship U.S.S. *Maine* steamed into harbor at Havana on a courtesy visit to Cuba. A few nights later, as the ship lay at anchor with most of its 354 officers and crew asleep below decks, the *Maine* exploded. Some 266 men died.

As cables and telegrams reached the United States, Americans were horrified. The *Maine*'s captain called for calm, but the yellow press pounded out papers as fast as their typesetters' hands could fly. Surely, they claimed, Spanish spies had planted a bomb aboard the *Maine*. The banner headline on the *Journal* screamed: THE WARSHIP MAINE

CREATE A ZEN GARDEN

THE ANCIENT kingdom of Japan was closed to foreigners until 1854. Once Western people were permitted into the island kingdom, they were amazed at Japanese gardens that had no plants—only rocks and sand.

However, these unusual gardens, called Zen gardens, are cultivated carefully to offer visitors a place to meditate and think quietly. From time to time, Zen gardeners rake the sand or soil in their gardens into different patterns in order to inspire new ways of thought.

You can create a small Zen garden in a dish to sit on a table. Then you can rearrange it any way you like. Which patterns help you feel a sense of peace and quiet?

You'll Need
❖ Large, shallow dish or pan
❖ Sand or fine soil
❖ Fork (the larger the better)
❖ Unusual rocks, shells, sticks or other natural materials

Scout around indoors and out for some unusual items for your garden. You can include small things you have picked up on the beach, in the woods, or along a stream.

Pour the sand into the dish so that it's about half full. Then arrange your found objects in a pattern that pleases you when you look at it.

Finally, use the tines of the fork to rake a pattern into the sand and around your display.

Depending on your mood, you may change the rocks in your garden as you wish. Play around with patterns in the sand, too. Do you find yourself simply "enjoying the moment" as you work in your Zen garden?

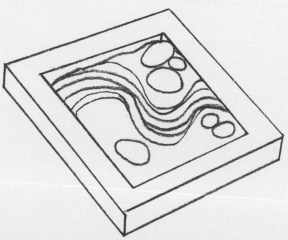

WAS SPLIT IN TWO BY AN ENEMY'S SECRET INFERNAL MACHINE.

War with Spain seemed certain, but still President McKinley tried to avoid it. The president, who had seen plenty of death in the Civil War, did not want a new one. He stalled preparations for battle as he waited to learn for certain who sank the *Maine*. The delay infuriated Roosevelt. The president, he sputtered, "has no more backbone than a chocolate éclair."

Roosevelt worried because the navy's Asia fleet, commanded by the brilliant Commodore James Dewey, sat in Hong Kong. American warships lay entirely too far away to attack the Spanish fleet that blocked the harbor of Manila in the Philippine Islands.

The situation frustrated Roosevelt, but he was only assistant secretary of the navy, with no authority to act—until Secretary Long decided to take a half day off from work. That's when Roosevelt pounced. In just one afternoon, he issued a flurry of orders to move ships, order ammunition, and find more sailors. Roosevelt wrote a fateful cable to Commodore Dewey: KEEP FULL OF COAL. IN THE EVENT DECLARATION OF WAR [ON] SPAIN, YOUR DUTY WILL BE TO SEE THAT THE SPANISH SQUADRON WILL NOT LEAVE.

Dewey complied and prepared his fleet to sail for Manila. When Secretary Long returned the next morning, he discovered that Roosevelt had "gone at things like a bull in a china shop." Roosevelt's afternoon as boss put the navy on a war footing.

Events ran wild as the yellow press called for a war of independence to free Cuba.

The Call

VOLUME LXXXIII.—NO. 86.   SAN FRANCISCO, THURSDAY, FEBRUARY 24, 1898.   PRICE FIVE CENTS.

AN OUTSIDE EXPLOSION WRECKED THE MAINE

EVIDENCE OF TREACHERY IS CONCLUSIVE

OFFICIALS NOW ALMOST CONCEDE IT

Grave Fear Spain Will Not Be Able to Punish the Guilty.

Upon the Strength of the Sagasta Ministry Will Depend the Contingency of War Between the Two Nations.

Copyrighted, 1898, by James Gordon Bennett.

HAVANA, Feb. 23.—There is now little doubt that the report of the board of inquiry investigating the cause of the wreck of the Maine will be to the effect that the prime cause of the explosion was a sub-

AN ABSURD RUMOR.

NEW YORK, Feb. 23.—A Washington special to the Herald says: Reports that Senator Proctor had gone to Cuba on a special mission for the President are officially and emphatically denied at the White House and the State Department. The Senator left here about a week ago for a fishing trip in Florida waters. He said at that time he might go to Havana if he could find some congenial friend to go with him. The authorities here do not know whether he has gone to Havana, and pronounce as absurd the statement that he is to meet General Lee for the purpose of bringing confidential reports to Washington. They can see no reason for making messenger-boys out of United States Senators, especially when Consul-General Lee could readily secure the detail of a naval officer if he wished to send anything he was afraid to trust to the regular channels.

official and conservative element prefers to not talk of war openly—at any rate, till there is proven good excuse for it, but Weyler's old officers and friends would welcome war with the United States. Captain-General Blanco wants peace, but he is placed in a very trying position. If foul

RETIRED OFFICERS SUMMONED.

PHILADELPHIA, Feb. 23.—Following the report that an order had been received at the United States Embassy at London, directing all officers of the United States at present in England on leave to return to their ships at once, it was learned to-day that all retired naval officers of the United States have received notice from Secretary Long, directing them to place themselves in communication with the Navy Department.

A retired naval officer of this city, who has served under Admiral Farragut, said that the notice applied to about 300 naval officers throughout the country on the retired list. It was of a confidential nature, but its provisions were to the effect that officers under 62 years of age who could pass a physical examination showing themselves to be fit for duty would be required to hold themselves in readiness for service at a moment's notice from Washington.

All who received the communication were asked to acknowledge its receipt immediately, giving any prospective change of address, and placing themselves unreservedly at the disposal of the Government.

The United States Lighthouse Tender Mangrove, on Board of Which the Maine Board of Inquiry Is Conducting Its Investigations in Havana Harbor.

THE MONTGOMERY ORDERED TO SAIL TO CUBA'S CAPITAL

She Will Take the Place of the Ill-Fated Maine in the Harbor of the Hostile City of Havana.

are centered, the eyes of the civilized world, will probably conclude its work in Havana to-morrow night, or Friday at the latest. Its conclusion will be unanimous, the court being composed of three members apart from its judge-advocate, Lieutenant - Commander Marix, under the...

to be heard on that point already made by divers who are regularly enlisted men in the naval arm of the Government service than upon any testimony that might be given by men who, however expert they may be, are the employes of a private corporation unconnected with the naval department except...

TAMPA, Fla., Feb. 23.—The United States cruiser Montgomery, Commander Converse, arrived at Port Tampa at 9 o'clock this morning and Captain Crowninshield, Chief of the Bureau of Navigation, who was on board, left at once for Washington.

aground on a sand bar, but was got off without sustaining any damage.

WASHINGTON, Feb. 23.—Simultaneously with the departure of the Texas and Washville from Galveston for Key West the Marblehead will leave New Orleans and the Detroit will leave Mobile for Key West. These

The *San Francisco Call* headline blamed Spain for blowing up the *Maine*. Today, historians offer differing ideas.

OLD INSULT, YUMMY DESSERT!

THEODORE ROOSEVELT criticized President McKinley for not standing up to the Spanish government. He said that McKinley had "no more backbone than a chocolate éclair."

What an insult! However, soft creamy éclairs, with gooey insides, are delicious.

You can make a simple version of éclairs in layers in a pan. Whip some up—and discover what Roosevelt was talking about.

Adult supervision required

You'll Need

Utensils

- 9" x 13" rectangular pan
- Saucepan
- Wooden spoon
- Pot holders
- Plastic wrap

Cream Puff Bottom Layer

- 1 cup water
- ¼ teaspoon salt
- ½ cup (1 stick) real butter
- 1 cup flour
- 4 eggs

Filling

- 2 boxes (3 oz.) instant French vanilla pudding mix
- 1 teaspoon vanilla
- 2¼ cups cold milk
- 12 oz. container of refrigerated whipped topping
- Chocolate syrup

Before you begin to cook, grease and flour the baking pan by rubbing a little bit of butter all over the inside of the pan. Spoon some flour into the pan and shake the pan until the sides are coated lightly with flour. Shake the extra flour out of the pan. Set the pan aside.

Pour the water into the saucepan and stir in the salt and butter. Heat the water, salt, and butter just until the water boils and the butter melts. Remove the pan from the heat.

Use the wooden spoon to stir in the flour all at once. The flour will start to blend with the water.

Then break each egg and stir it into the mixture, one egg at a time. Beat the mixture with the wooden spoon after you add each egg. The mixture should be thick and glossy—and very hard to stir.

Spread the mixture all over the bottom of the baking pan until it is level. Use the back of a spoon to help you.

Put the pan in the oven and bake at 400°F for 45 to 50 minutes. Start to check the puff when it's baked for 40 minutes. The puff should be golden brown, cooked through but not overbaked.

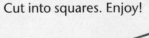

Let the puff cool completely.

Blend both boxes of pudding mix with milk and vanilla thoroughly until the mixture sets up. Then carefully fold in the container of whipped topping using gentle strokes with a big spoon. You should have a light, airy mixture.

Drop large spoonfuls of the pudding-topping mixture on top of the puff layer. Then use the back of the spoon to spread the mixture evenly all over.

Drizzle chocolate syrup all over the pudding-topping layer. Refrigerate it for at least two hours. If you cover it with plastic wrap, be aware that it might stick to the top of the dessert.

Cut into squares. Enjoy!

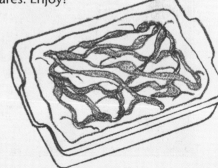

Unfortunately, the jungle hid the enemy just as well. Without warning, a band of Spanish gunmen launched a surprise attack as rifle bullets whizzed overhead. They made "a nasty, malicious little noise," wrote a reporter who fought with Roosevelt. The Rough Riders returned fire with their fast-action carbines. They began to move forward, and for the moment, the Spanish retreated.

The Rough Riders had tasted blood. Eight of their own lay dead from the ambush, with another 31 wounded. As they waited for

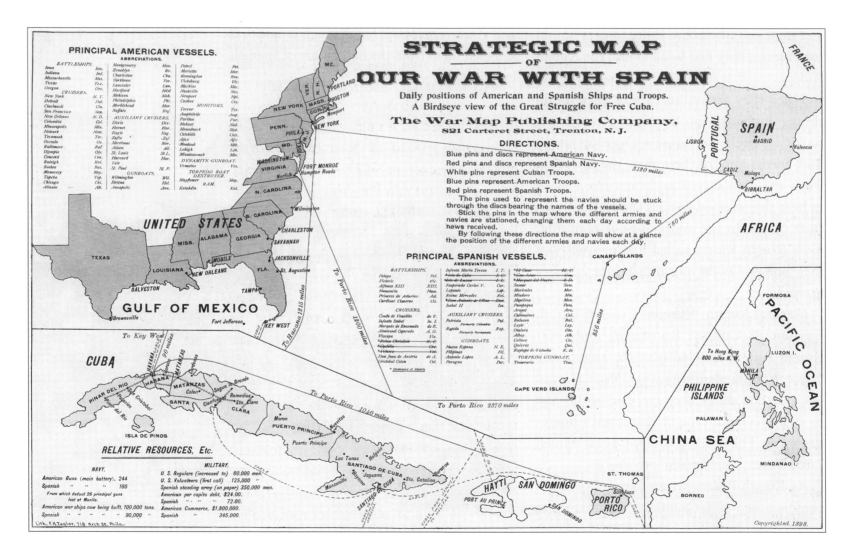

orders, Roosevelt and his men buried their friends before the vultures could get to them. Then the Rough Riders hid in the jungle heat awaiting the order to push forward and attack.

They waited for days for an order that didn't come. Rain poured on the men, and they were hungry. Roosevelt blamed the poor planning squarely on the general who had ordered the attack but who stayed safe, far from the front. Furious, Roosevelt took it on himself to backtrack to a supply depot. There, he got into an argument with a quartermaster before rounding up 1,100 pounds of beans for his men.

Though their enthusiasm for battle never faltered, the Rough Riders struggled. None of these gringos (as the Cubans called the Americans) was prepared for the exhausting heat and humidity of tropical Cuba in the summertime. Secretary Long had spoken of Roosevelt "brushing mosquitoes from his neck," but no one could foresee how their bites would infect and kill full-grown men.

Besides malaria from mosquitos and yellow fever, dirty drinking water sickened them, too, as they fell ill to typhoid fever and gut-draining diarrhea. A senior officer farther up in the command took sick, and Colonel Wood left to replace him. Thanks to a mosquito, Theodore Roosevelt was now a full colonel and commander of the Rough Riders.

"My Crowded Hour"

On June 30 the order to move finally came, and the Rough Riders slid eight miles inland to the spot from where they would attack the next day, July 1, 1898. Most of the men had shed their heavy blue uniform jackets and wore shirts and sombreros with their pants.

When the attack began, Spanish fire pinned down the Rough Riders in tall grass. As Roosevelt checked on his soldiers and issued orders, men around him were gunned down. His favorite captain, a sheriff named Bucky O'Neill, caught a bullet through the mouth and died before he knew what hit him.

No sooner had O'Neill fallen than orders arrived: Roosevelt and the Rough Riders should join the rest of the cavalry for an attack on Kettle Hill. (The hill took its name from giant pots used for cooking the sugar cane that sat at the top.) Roosevelt's troopers began to move forward. As he sat astride Little Texas, Roosevelt waved a pistol reclaimed from the *Maine* and urged his men on.

Since he was riding the only horse in the troop, Roosevelt made a ready target for Spanish snipers. Roosevelt seemed not to care about his own safety as he rode up and down the line of soldiers, urging them on to take the hill. As they moved forward, the Rough

Riders mingled with soldiers of the Ninth Cavalry, a troop of black soldiers.

Soon the patchwork army of "[w]hite regiments, black regiments, Regulars and Rough Riders, representing the young manhood of the North and South, fought shoulder to shoulder" in the charge up Kettle Hill. Their inspiration was a squat-bodied colonel who wore spectacles tied to his head.

Richard Harding Davis, a dashing reporter with the *New York Times*, told the story:

Colonel Roosevelt, on horseback, broke from the woods behind the line of the Ninth, and finding its men lying in his way, shouted: "If you don't wish to go forward, let my men pass, please." The junior officers of the Ninth, with their Negroes, instantly sprang into line with the Rough Riders, and charged at the blue block-house on the right.

I speak of Roosevelt first because… he was, without doubt, the most conspicuous figure in the charge…. Roosevelt, mounted high on horseback, and charging the rifle-pits at a gallop and quite alone, made you feel that you would like to cheer. He wore on his sombrero a blue polka-dot handkerchief… which, as he advanced, floated out straight behind his head, like a guidon [small flag].

As they came to the crest of the hill, Roosevelt dismounted and joined the rest of his troopers on foot. Some of the men stabbed the ground with their flags.

But there was another hill to go. Roosevelt called for his men to follow and began a charge toward San Juan Hill. But when he turned to look behind him, only a handful followed. The rest hadn't heard his orders.

Roosevelt turned back to gather his troopers. This time, they heard his command to capture San Juan Hill. As Roosevelt and his aide pushed up the second hill, two Spaniards fired directly at them. Roosevelt fired back and killed one, who "doubled up like a jack-rabbit." The American forces overwhelmed the Spanish, and they backed away in full retreat. The Americans, now in charge of the hills above Santiago, were ordered to wait.

On July 4, the 122nd anniversary of the Declaration of Independence, the army got a gift from the navy when it destroyed Spain's Atlantic squadron of ships in Havana Harbor. On July 17, with its ships destroyed and key city under siege, Spain surrendered.

On August 12, Spain accepted an agreement to free Cuba. Spain also transferred colonies to the United States: Puerto Rico, Guam, and the Philippines.

On that day, the United States of America became a worldwide empire—thanks to, as

Secretary of State John Hay put it, "a splendid little war."

Rough Times for Rough Riders

THOUGH THE Spanish had surrendered, the Rough Riders did not receive army orders to go home, and so they stayed in Cuba. Man after man caught yellow fever, and there was no sign that Roosevelt's soldiers could leave. Roosevelt cabled the War Department in Washington to protest, but the army stayed silent. A commander suggested that Roosevelt's men weren't ill with fever but simply homesick.

Again, the outraged Roosevelt took action. "He tried to feed them," a reporter wrote. "He helped build latrines. He cursed the quartermasters and the 'dogs' on the transports [ships], to get quinine [medicine] and grub for them."

Roosevelt broke every army rule, especially when he leaked the news to the press and embarrassed Secretary of War Russell Alger. Once newspapers broke the story about dead and dying men in Santiago, the army ordered the soldiers home.

Secretary Alger, however, took his revenge. Theodore Roosevelt's leadership during the campaign had earned him a nomination for

"Colonel Roosevelt" and his Rough Riders became heroes in American plays and songs after they helped defeat the Spanish in Cuba. Library of Congress LC-USZ62-26060

the Congressional Medal of Honor, but Alger made sure that Roosevelt never received it.

Nonetheless, Theodore Roosevelt had won his war. The American people needed a hero. And now the Republicans knew just who should run in the race for governor of New York.

An Unexpected President

6

BARELY SIX weeks after he came home from Cuba, Theodore Roosevelt won the Republican nomination for New York governor. He campaigned from the back of a train, the *Roosevelt Special*, on a whistle-stop tour to meet New Yorkers.

As always, Roosevelt had to play politics. Tom Platt, known as the Easy Boss, ran the Republican Party in Roosevelt's home state. Platt had no use for Roosevelt, war hero or not. Platt could not stop the public outcry for Roosevelt, but he made things difficult. Besides, the current governor, a Republican, was deep in scandals. Many Republicans threatened to cross party lines and vote for the Democrats' candidate, Judge Augustus Van Wyck.

"I am not having an entirely pleasant campaign," Roosevelt remarked.

Experience in New York's General Assembly, and again as police commissioner, had taught Theodore Roosevelt the art of politics. Now he worked the New York election like a master. Roosevelt rounded up some loyal Rough Riders to shake hands with voters as they whistle-stopped across the state. He also pointed fingers at Democrats in Tammany Hall for trying to bribe a judge.

The Republicans had an uphill battle, but many New Yorkers liked Roosevelt's straight talk. He managed to squeak by Van Wyck in the November election. With his family watching, Roosevelt was inaugurated as New York's governor in Albany on January 2, 1899, a day so cold the band couldn't play its frozen instruments.

At the young age of 40, Theodore Roosevelt held one of the most powerful political jobs in America. Cartoonists enjoyed drawing him and often tagged him as "TR."

Roosevelt did not enjoy "an entirely pleasant" governorship, either. Platt was determined to block Roosevelt as he tried to reform New York's corrupt government. The governor and the Easy Boss argued about everything.

Roosevelt refused to accept Platt's choice to head New York's canal system. Roosevelt also backed an unpopular idea to cut state employee's work days to just eight hours. Roosevelt the outdoorsman signed laws to ban sawmills from dumping their waste water into streams. He also tried to beef up New York's forest, fish, and game commissions.

For Platt, even worse was Roosevelt's call to tax public companies—utilities—that pumped natural gas and water to homes and businesses. Platt complained as Roosevelt "clinched his fist and gritted his teeth" to force the new tax through the New York Assembly.

As Roosevelt got used to his new office, he and Platt came to an uneasy truce. Every time an important job opened up, Roosevelt would send a list of handpicked nominees for Platt to make a final choice. Some New Yorkers complained that Roosevelt catered too much to the Easy Boss. Yet Roosevelt pointed out that it was better to reform the Republican Party by working with insiders. To compromise, he felt, was both practical and effective.

Governor Roosevelt looked at big business with growing doubts. All over America, businesses linked into giant monopolies, called trusts, in order to squash their competitors.

Roosevelt did not trust the trusts. As he went after the utilities in New York State, Theodore Roosevelt operated with a sense of fair play. To Roosevelt a company wasn't bad simply because it was big. He watched carefully as the captains of industry played their games. If they played squarely, that was fine. But if dishonesty was their style, he cried foul. Roosevelt summed up his strategy against his opponents when he wrote to a friend, "I have always been fond of the West African proverb: 'Speak softly and carry a big stick; you will go far.'"

Summer at Sagamore Hill

OF ANY spot in the wide world he traveled, Theodore Roosevelt loved Sagamore Hill the best. Joyous days unfolded there during long hot summers, when the family tramped down from their hilltop home for swims in Oyster Bay or outings in the rowboat as Theodore manned the oars. The children screamed with laughter—or fear—when Theodore tossed them off a floating dock to force them to

Theodore Roosevelt's "big stick" declaration became a legend. A cartoonist used it to poke fun at Roosevelt when he was president in 1906. Library of Congress
LC-USZ62-42035

learn how to swim. When everyone jumped in at once in a game called stagecoach, Theodore made sure that "the number of heads that came up corresponded with the number of children who had gone down."

Visits from numbers of Roosevelt cousins and friends made things merrier. The big shingled house shook as little feet pounded up and down staircases and across its wooden floors. On rare days, among the guests was the Roosevelt children's cousin, Eleanor Roosevelt. Eleanor was one of the visitors who hated to jump off the floating dock. Theodore's niece, a brilliant but awkward girl, was living a quiet, sad life. To visit Sagamore was a treasure, because Eleanor adored her "Uncle Theodore."

Sagamore Hill on a postage stamp. Theodore Roosevelt's words say it best: "At Sagamore Hill, we love a great many things—birds and trees and books, and all things beautiful, and horses and rifles and children and hard work and the joy of life."

MAKE A CAMPAIGN BUTTON

THEODORE ROOSEVELT ran for elected office seven times in his life. Each time he threw himself wholeheartedly into campaigning. Campaign buttons in those days ranged from simple pins to true works of art. Some were designed to look like broaches or cameos and worn like jewelry. You can design a cool-looking button to show your support for a candidate for student government, state governor, even president of the United States!

This campaign button appeared when Theodore Roosevelt ran for governor.

Adult supervision required

You'll Need
- ❖ 1 bottle cap, any size
- ❖ 1 sheet white or colored paper
- ❖ Pencil
- ❖ Scissors
- ❖ Magazines or computer with color printer
- ❖ Clear tape
- ❖ Crystal lacquer or other clear craft lacquer (available at craft stores)
- ❖ Hot glue gun
- ❖ Safety pin

1. Put the bottle cap on the sheet of paper with the top (flat) side down. Trace around the cap with a pencil.

2. Cut out the circle you just traced, cutting just inside your pencil mark. Fit the paper circle inside the bottle cap. In order for it to fit neatly, you may need to trim the edges of the circle a bit. Once you have a snug fit, remove the paper circle.

3. Think about what you want your button to say. Then write out your campaign slogan, like "Vote for Ava," using letters or words cut from magazines or typed on your computer and printed out with a color printer. You may need to experiment with type sizes. Cut out your words and tape them onto the paper circle.

4. Cover the paper circle completely with clear tape on both sides. (This will keep words and colors from "bleeding" and looking fuzzy

continued . . .

when the lacquer is applied.) Trim any excess tape from around the edges.

5. Put a drop of crystal lacquer inside the bottle cap. Spread it evenly with the tip of the bottle, being careful not to get any on your fingers. Place your paper circle over the lacquer, slogan side up, and press to secure.

6. Fill the bottle cap to the top edges with crystal lacquer. The lacquer will appear cloudy at first but will dry clear within 24 hours. Let the cap sit undisturbed overnight.

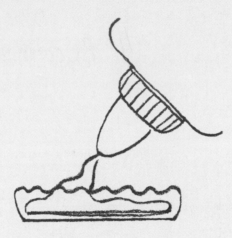

7. Ask a parent or other adult to help you with the hot glue gun. The adult should heat up the glue gun and put a drop on the back, or flat side, of the bottle cap. You can then press your open safety pin down into the hot glue, horizontal to your slogan, with the open side of the pin up. Let it sit and harden for about an hour. Pin your new button to your shirt or backpack and wear it proudly!

When Theodore was governor of New York in 1900, the Fourth of July began at 4:00 A.M. "by the thoughtfulness of some youngster with a bunch of giant fire-crackers." Theodore was ill, sick yet again with a bout of Cuban fever—malaria. Nonetheless, the father knew his duty and supervised 17 children all morning, "keeping the punk-sticks [sparklers] lighted and forestalling casualties."

In the afternoon, the family took a break and went into Oyster Bay to hear the town's clergymen make patriotic speeches. However, the most distinguished orator that day was the governor of New York, Theodore himself.

Just as the Oyster Bay band played "Hail Columbia!" Governor Roosevelt arrived to the town square. He made a grand speech to people dressed in their Sunday best, both plainspoken farmers who rode in open wagons and "swells" in their "high traps, some drawn by four horses."

Men wore starched collars; women dressed for summer in crisp white skirts, blouses, and straw hats. Girls in white dresses trimmed with ribbons drank pink lemonade, while

ABOVE RIGHT: Sagamore Hill in 1918.
Sagamore Hill National Historic Site, National Park Service

RIGHT: Theodore Roosevelt probably took this photo of Ethel, Edith, Kermit, Ted, and Alice Roosevelt at play near Sagamore Hill.
Theodore Roosevelt Collection, Harvard University Library

William McKinley and Theodore Roosevelt appeared on an early campaign pin designed to work like a real button.

The job of vice president of the United States, as Platt and Roosevelt knew, was nearly laughable. The president held all the power. No vice president had ever gone on to be elected president of the United States. Roosevelt fought the idea of becoming vice president; he wanted to stay on as governor. But behind closed doors, other powerful men, each for his own political gain, plotted to give the nomination to Roosevelt.

When Roosevelt strode down the aisle at the Republican convention in Philadelphia in June 1900, he wore his Rough Riders hat, and the crowd went wild. Roosevelt agonized over the offer, but events hurled his nomination forward. In the end, every man in the hall except Roosevelt voted for him to run with President McKinley.

Mark Hanna, McKinley's close friend and boss of the Republican Party, turned to the rest of his group. Fuming, he asked, "Don't any of you realize that there's only one life between that madman and the presidency?"

As was the custom, President McKinley did not travel to meet voters, but he campaigned from his front porch in Ohio. Roosevelt, though, crisscrossed the nation by rail. Until Election Day in November, he traveled 21,000 miles to rally voters against William Jennings Bryan, again the Democrats' man. The Republicans swept the election; the American people stood firm behind the party that had thrust the United States onto the world stage.

On March 4, 1901, Theodore Roosevelt was inaugurated vice president of the United States. In spite of his lofty title, the new vice president did not plan on having much to do except preside over the Senate when it met. On March 5 he entered the Senate chamber to oversee a special session for the next five days. Then Congress recessed, and everyone left Washington for the summer. Congress would not return until December.

Determined to stay busy, Roosevelt gathered books so that he could fill empty hours by studying law. But friends were already looking ahead to the next election, saying that he was a shoo-in for the presidential nomination in 1904.

The Roosevelts settled into summer days at Sagamore Hill, and Theodore made several trips to Minnesota, Illinois, and Colorado to give speeches and meet Americans one-on-one. If Roosevelt was going to be the Republicans' man in 1904, it was vital for him to meet as many voters as he could.

Then, all too soon, the summer of 1901 drew to an end. Young Ted left for boarding school as Edith and the smaller children packed up for camp in the Adirondack Mountains to escape Oyster Bay's sticky air.

President McKinley and Vice President Roosevelt resumed their official duties. Roosevelt headed to Lake Champlain to a meeting of the Vermont Fish and Game League. The president, meanwhile, journeyed to Buffalo to tour the Pan American Exposition, an international fair celebrating the Americas.

On September 6, the final day of his visit, McKinley was shaking hands with visitors when a young man who appeared to have an injured right hand came to greet him. But in his handkerchief-wrapped hand, the young man hid a gun, and he shot the president point-blank twice. Shocked Americans found out that the assassin was an anarchist, a terrorist who wanted to wipe out civilized government.

McKinley was rushed to a hospital for surgery. Once his doctors had finished, the president was taken to a private home. The doctors felt that McKinley was out of danger and would recover.

A telephone call to Roosevelt told him of the shooting. Without delay, he hurried across Lake Champlain by boat to catch a special train to Buffalo. There, the vice president and members of McKinley's cabinet waited for news. It seemed that McKinley was recovering nicely. The president's doctors assured Roosevelt that he could leave Buffalo to return to his family in the Adirondacks.

School Days

For the most part, the Roosevelt children accepted moving from school to school as part of the family routine. Sometimes, however, Alice fought the changes. When her father governed New York from the state capitol in Albany, she found life there boring.

Her parents enrolled her at a boarding school in New York City for young ladies of good background. Alice, always the rebel, threatened that if she were forced to go, she would misbehave. After many battles, her parents relented. Alice stayed in Albany, where she and Ethel did lessons with their governess.

Ted, Kermit, Archie, and Quentin went to public school in Oyster Bay, Albany, and Washington. When Ted was 13 in the fall of 1900, he left for Groton, an elite prep school in Massachusetts. There he studied to enter Harvard University—as would Kermit, Archie, and Quentin.

The Roosevelt Children in 1899. Left to right: Ethel, Ted, Alice, Quentin, Kermit, and Archie. Sagamore Hill National Historical Site, National Park Service

When Roosevelt became president, Ethel boarded at the elite Cathedral School in Washington on weeknights and came home on weekends. By the time they were 18, Alice and Ethel had finished their formal education. In those days most girls, even upper-class young ladies of Alice's and Ethel's circle, did not see a need to go to college.

Three days later, McKinley's condition reversed. The president was dying, and officials started the tricky process of getting

Vice President Roosevelt back to Buffalo. "Then began a vigorous effort to annihilate time and space," wrote Ansley Wilcox, who opened his home to Roosevelt. It took two hours just to reach the vice president's secretary, William Loeb, by telephone. Wilcox learned that Roosevelt's camp lay "some hours beyond the end of the rail and telegraph lines." Vice President Roosevelt was out of touch.

Roosevelt, in fact, was on top of a mountain that he had climbed on a dark, rainy day. As he came down with his fellow climbers, a runner rushed up the trail with telegrams bearing bad news. Roosevelt slid in the mud down the rest of mountain and hiked 12 miles to the nearest telephone. At ten o'clock that night, when he knew that the president lay near death, Roosevelt left the Adirondacks.

All night long, he and a driver traveled "on a wild ride of forty miles by buckboard [an open wagon]" on slippery trails along cliffs and valleys, with only a small lantern to light their way. Every so often, they stopped to get a fresh team of horses, but there was no new word about the president.

At dawn, Roosevelt finally reached a railway station, where a special train waited. Loeb handed him a telegram telling Roosevelt what he did not want to hear. McKinley had died at 2:15 that morning.

Theodore Roosevelt was now President of the United States.

When he reached Buffalo at 1:34 that afternoon, Roosevelt went by carriage to Wilcox's home. There he changed out of his traveling suit into a long frock coat and striped trousers borrowed from his host. Someone appeared with a top hat, and Roosevelt felt

Although Tom Platt was Theodore Roosevelt's political rival, Platt kept an album with photos of the Roosevelts. This one shows Roosevelt talking to reporters after President McKinley's shooting.
Theodore Roosevelt Collection Harvard University Library

properly dressed for the sad but historic tasks at hand.

Roosevelt called on Mrs. McKinley and family friends, including Mark Hanna, at the private residence where they stayed hidden from the public. In a darkened room, he paid his respects to the dead president. That duty completed, Roosevelt returned to Ansley Wilcox's home. There, surrounded by most of the dead president's cabinet, other officials, and a few reporters, Theodore Roosevelt took the presidential oath of office. The simple ceremony moved quickly. At the end, he added, "This do I swear." No photographs were allowed. The next morning, pencil sketches of the ceremony, drawn from eyewitness accounts of the event, appeared in newspapers across the shocked nation.

Ansley Wilcox took a lesson about American democracy from events that day. "It takes less in the way of ceremony to make a president in this country, than it does to make a king in England or any monarchy, but the significance of the event is no less great."

Going (Sometimes) Slowly

REPUBLICANS IN Washington fretted about the new president. The power players were a good 20 years older than Roosevelt, who at 42 was the youngest president ever in the White House. His bold ways and knack for straight talk worried them. Roosevelt, a product of his generation, embodied many progressive ideas. He championed reforms in government to improve the everyday lives of ordinary Americans.

Mark Hanna counseled Roosevelt to go slowly with any changes to McKinley's programs. Roosevelt agreed to Hanna's suggestions—but only as far as he could keep the nation in balance.

Balance seemed to be the key theme of Roosevelt's first address to Congress in January 1902. The new young president had big business to satisfy, as well as the demands of labor groups and working people. He had to please isolationists by thinking about America's problems at home. At the same time, he needed to help the growing nation face the challenges of becoming a global player.

Then Roosevelt got word that big businessmen were playing a new game of monopoly, this time with American railroads. The players were John Pierpont Morgan, the New York industrialist who owned the Northern Pacific Railway, and James J. Hill, the brilliant railroad man who engineered the rise of the Great Northern Railway.

Through clever purchases of smaller rail lines and outright dirty dealing, Morgan and Hill created the Northern Securities

An elegant image of the president appeared on a British cigarette card.

Company. The conglomerate joined the brand new U.S. Steel Corporation to become one of the nation's largest monopolies. Morgan and Hill controlled all the transportation from Chicago—crossroads of America's railway system—to San Francisco, Portland, and Seattle. From there, they could control markets in China and Japan that glittered with the promise of even more riches.

Not so fast, President Roosevelt said. In and of themselves, giant companies were fine, as long as they played fairly in the markets. But big monopolies such as the Northern Securities Company abused their power by blocking competition from other railway haulers. To Roosevelt, a conglomerate was bad if it did not do the public good. This giant company represented the worst kind of monopoly. Morgan and Hill, the president declared, were acting like tyrants.

The president ordered U.S. Attorney General Philander Knox to dissolve the company. To do so, Knox applied an existing law called the Sherman Anti-Trust Act. He accused the Northern Securities trust of blocking fair trade. Morgan and Hill fought the government's lawsuit all the way to the U.S. Supreme Court, where they lost in March 1904. Not only had they restrained trade, the Court declared, they had blocked free competition.

Theodore Roosevelt had made his move as a trust buster. The demands of coal miners, hundreds of whom were dying every year, came next.

Taking on Big Coal

THE COAL fields of Pennsylvania, Ohio, Indiana, and Illinois rumbled with troubling news. The nation's miners were about to go on strike. The 140,000 miners, from smooth-skinned boys to worn-out old men, held rightful grudges against the mine operators. They worked 10 to 12 hours every day for 6 days a week. They had gone without pay raises for 20 years. And mine owners typically cheated them when they did pay. Miners were paid by the ton for the coal they dug—and the mine operators called a ton anything from 2,340 to even 4,000 pounds, which is two tons.

The coal barons who owned the mines had one of the worst names among American industrialists. George Baer, one of the barons, trampled on the rights of his miners. Baer declared that God himself gave "control of the property interests of the country" to the owners—not the workers. Even men of influence, including J. P. Morgan and Mark Hanna, could not stomach Baer's conceit.

The strike dragged on all summer. The mine owners refused to meet with John

Mitchell, the head of the United Mine Workers union. Autumn came, and coal prices skyrocketed as the nation's supply dwindled.

In Washington the president fumed as visitors came and letters arrived calling for him to act. After all, coal fueled the nation's factories, warmed its homes, and powered its navy. The prospect of a coal famine, as the president called it, demanded action. But as he combed through the Constitution, Roosevelt could not find a principle that allowed him, the president of the United States, to end the strike.

The president shook his big stick in a clever way. He named a commission to hear both sides of the argument and declare a settlement. Then the president appointed an army general to marshal a force of 10,000 soldiers. Their job, stated Roosevelt, would be to run the mines if the owners did not settle the strike.

The owners still defied Roosevelt and refused to negotiate as long as a "labor man" sat on the commission. On October 15 the president and his aides stayed up all night on the telephone to get the mine operators to negotiate. At long last, the frustrated Roosevelt figured out that the mulish owners didn't care if a labor man sat on the commission—just as long as he wasn't *called* a labor man.

That was fine with Roosevelt. What was the difference "between Tweedledum and Tweedledee?" he asked, picturing the twins whom Alice met in *Through the Looking Glass*. The strikers went back to their jobs as the commission did its work. Over time, the miners won a 10 percent raise, a nine-hour work day, and the right to watch coal being weighed. For their part, the owners raised coal prices by 10 percent—and still refused to recognize the miners' union.

Workers as young as eight years old, called breaker boys, shuffled their feet through chutes of coal in order to pick out slate and debris from the coal. Library of Congress LC-USZC4-2322

Sick Rooms

All the Roosevelt children had their bouts of illness and broken bones. Even during the drama of Theodore's rise to the presidency, Edith had to care for Archie, whose tonsils swelled with pain, and Quentin, who had an earache. (A trip to the doctor turned up a pebble in Quentin's ear.) At the same time, Alice was recovering from a hit in the mouth, her teeth shaken loose. Doctors wanted to pull them and make her dentures. Fortunately, Edith said no, and Alice kept her teeth.

When they lived in the White House, measles ran through the children and each had to stay in bed for days. When Archie felt better and started getting bored, Quentin decided to cheer him up. Quentin enlisted a White House servant to help, and the pair smuggled Archie's pony, Algonquin, up the elevator for a visit.

During his first winter at Groton, Ted got sick with double pneumonia, and his temperature soared to 105 degrees. Edith rushed from the White House. Worried, the president boarded his private railroad car, hitched to its own steam engine, and joined her at Ted's bedside. Headlines said it all:

THEODORE ROOSEVELT, JR., HAS DOUBLE PNEUMONIA
President's Family Physician Summoned from New York.
Doctors Resort to Oxygen Treatment—
Make No Statement as to
Boy's Chances, But Await
the Crisis.

No medicines had been discovered that could cure Ted. Like any other parents, Theodore and Edith had to wait as the disease ran its course. When the president finally left the infirmary to talk with reporters, they knew Ted would survive.

Theodore Roosevelt scored a victory as president. He had used his executive power to end the coal strike. Some asked whether he acted without the proper authority. But the president saw himself as a steward of the public good and had his answer ready.

"The Constitution was made for the people and not the people for the Constitution!"

The president oversaw the coal crisis from a wheelchair. In September, as he paid a visit to Boston, his carriage crashed into a trolley, and a Secret Service agent riding beside the driver was killed. The carriage overturned, cutting the president's head and slashing his leg.

In usual form, Roosevelt carried on with a bandaged leg until the wound festered and infection spread to the bone. By then, three weeks had passed. The president, now on another trip, had surgery in Indianapolis—with only a local painkiller—to drain the wound.

Back in Washington, the president rested, but his leg refused to heal, and he returned for more surgery. This time, his doctors had to scrape the president's shin bone clear of infection. To block the pain, they used cocaine, a favorite medicine in Roosevelt's time that was later outlawed.

Roosevelt's leg never fully healed, but this he rarely let on. Those who watched carefully, however, could see that his leg pained him whenever he grew tired. It would trouble him the rest of his life.

The "President's Palace"

IN OCTOBER 1901 the Roosevelt family moved into their new home, the Executive Mansion. Theodore, Edith, Alice, Ethel, Kermit, Archie, and Quentin squeezed into the family living quarters on the second floor. Soon the Roosevelts found themselves fighting for space with the president's staff. All that separated them was a wall across a hallway.

When a friend came to call on the president, he found chaos in the old building.

I sat in the hall upstairs, waiting till he [Roosevelt] could see me; and around me a set of typewriters were clicking, and a set of clerks buzzing, and ink pots, and waste baskets; I seem also to remember spittoons, and a great ugly door with a window of frosted glass cut this upper hall in two. It was a nasty place to be the First House in the Land.

The Executive Mansion had fallen into a disgraceful state. Whenever guests gathered in the East Room, servants had to prop up the floor to keep it from falling in. The building cried out to be rid of its Victorian gloom. As Alice recalled:

There was much plush and gilt and heavy upholstery, and the ceilings were frescoed with acres of oilcloth patterns. The length of the East Room was punctuated by three upholstered circular seats… out of which sprouted a potted palm. When the palms were removed, a not-too-large child could crouch in vacant space and pop out at passers-by.

The Roosevelts, living in a brand new century, needed a nicer place to live, conduct political affairs, and entertain, even if that meant doing away with hiding places for their children.

Under Edith's tasteful eye, architects planned changes to "restore the mansion to its colonial simplicity," the *New York Times* reported. The next summer, rebuilding began. The president's offices moved out of the house to quarters in a newly built West Wing. The family spread across most of the second floor, with new tubs for the baths the children took before school each morning.

A new electric elevator added an up-to-date convenience, which the boys put to good use smuggling hidden treasures into their rooms.

This 1901 photo captured a clear shot of President Theodore Roosevelt working at his desk in the White House. Library of Congress LC-USZ62-64138

Outdoors, old glass hothouses gave way to flower gardens with a colonial feel. When the president needed a break from work, he joined his friends for a match on the new tennis court.

Downstairs, the East Room became a ballroom, and the State Dining Room was stripped of its tired-looking wallpaper and lined with wood paneling. Several trophies, the heads of animals that Theodore had hunted, adorned the walls. Furniture with simple lines, a throwback to the home's Federal beginnings, replaced the stodgy tables and chairs.

Roosevelt felt that the building was not just his home but a museum of America. He demanded that the designers use American themes. All went well until "the white marble mantels in the lobby" were replaced with "carved mahogany," as the *Times* said. The president was fine with the change. But when he laid eyes on the new mantels and saw lions' heads on them, he ordered new ones—carved with buffalo heads instead.

Now the building took its new, official name. There had been several over the years: the Executive Mansion, the President's House, and the President's Palace. Theodore Roosevelt decided, once and for all, what its name should be. The president ordered new writing paper engraved with his address. The letterhead said simply, The White House.

At Play in the White House

THEODORE ROOSEVELT was a "bully" father to his six children. No matter where he was— in an office in New York, Albany, or Washington—he set aside time to play. Important visitors to the White House noticed that at

A portrait of Theodore Roosevelt graced the White House lobby after the building was remodeled in 1902.
Library of Congress LC-DIG-ppmsca-11634

A Matter of Color

During Theodore Roosevelt's lifetime, most whites felt superior to people of other races. Matters between blacks and whites seemed especially hard, because many people of color had been held as slaves in the South. At best, most African Americans were seen as children who needed limits set on their jobs, schools, and neighborhoods. At worst, they were treated as subhuman simply because they were black.

Even open-minded whites did not believe that blacks as a group were ready for equality in political and business life. Because most blacks had little schooling, educated whites viewed them as second-class. However, middle- and upper-class whites viewed poor whites in much the same way.

Clearly, Theodore Roosevelt was a man of his times in matters between white America and everyone else. Roosevelt thought that some people of color were ready to take part in society as equals to educated whites but that most were not.

Nonetheless, Roosevelt tried to judge people as individuals. Just days after the Roosevelts moved into the White House, the president invited Booker T. Washington to dine. Roosevelt respected Washington, a black teacher at the

Tuskegee Institute in Alabama. As an enslaved child, Washington had waved palms to fan his master and mistress at their dinner table. He believed that the power of learning would allow former slaves to take their rightful place alongside white Americans.

A newspaperman glanced at Washington's name on the White House register and wrote about the dinner. Across the South, newspapers, politicians, and preachers expressed their anger—how dare the president invite a Negro to put his legs under the same table where Roosevelt's wife sat? A paper in Memphis screamed, "The most damnable outrage which has ever been perpetrated by any citizen of the United States was committed yesterday by the President."

Roosevelt defended his decision, but the situation did not make smart political sense. Booker T. Washington visited the White House again, but he was not invited to dinner.

This 1903 artwork gave newspaper readers an idea of the Roosevelt-Washington dinner. Many were shocked to see President Roosevelt sitting at the same dinner table as Booker T. Washington. However, the word "equality" on the tablecloth shows that the artist approved of the president's guest.

four o'clock, a small boy would often knock at the president's office door to remind him.

Most of the White House was a playground for the Roosevelt brood. Alice and the others stole trays from the kitchen and slid down its stairs. Kermit and Archie teetered on stilts across its broad halls, which also served as an indoor ball ground. Growling like a grizzly,

A Family Circus

No matter where the Roosevelts lived, there were dogs for romping and horses and ponies to ride. At Sagamore Hill, Little Texas, the president's famed bronco from the Battle of San Juan Heights, lived out his later years. A badger joined the family circus, but his ankle-biting habit earned him a new home in a zoo. An eagle, a mountain lion, and a bear cub also ended up at the zoo after proving to be too exotic for Sagamore Hill.

At the White House, kangaroo rats hopped across the breakfast table, and guinea pigs made their way into guests' pockets. One congressman found himself helping Quentin off with his coat, trying to coax a good-sized snake out of the boy's sleeve. The White House stables sheltered the president's carriage horses as well as the Roosevelt family's mounts. For Archie, there was the stunning calico pony named Algonquin, "the most absolute pet of them all," his father declared.

Three or four dogs always trailed the Roosevelts—among them Jack, Sailor Boy, Skip, and Pete. Another big male mutt, Susan, kept his name through a very long life only because Archie had picked it. After the Roosevelts left Washington, they brought along the coffin of Edith's favorite dog, Jack, to be reburied at Saga-

Archie, a staff member, Ethel, and their cousin Philip James Roosevelt, with their dogs. Theodore Roosevelt Collection, Harvard University Library

more Hill. When a pet met its end at the estate, everyone gathered to bury it in the pet cemetery near a boulder chiseled with the words FAITHFUL FRIENDS.

the president led his children on merry chases through the White House. In turn, the children laid in wait to attack their father with pillow fights that left their beds so messy the maids complained.

Theodore took his sons and male visitors on rambles through the woods. The boys ran barelegged in short pants that led to multiple mosquito bites and cases of poison ivy. (Theodore, a visitor sniffed, always wore long pants on these hikes.) Theodore sometimes charged outdoors in point-to-point "tramps," leading everyone in a straight line, no matter what kind of rock, fence, or stream blocked their way. Sometimes, when everyone was dressed up, the president would strip off every piece of clothing he wore when he crossed a river, and his guests followed suit.

On other days, clothes didn't matter: "[W]hen Father was President," Ted remembered, "we were tramping through the swamp that then lay to the south of the White House. A deep creek barred our way. We swam it, then we noticed that our clothes had a peculiar and offensive smell. It developed that we had unwittingly swam a drain."

The president of the United States had tramped his troop through an open sewer.

True to form, President Roosevelt "took exercise" whenever the weather was good. He and Edith rode their horses during Washington's late afternoons, the president on Bleistein and Edith on Yagenka. Bleistein, a hunter, was the president's favorite horse and was known to clear five-foot fences. Fifteen paces away, a member of the United States cavalry trailed the president. When Roosevelt abruptly left the main road and headed for fields and streams, it was the guard's job to follow as the president, aboard Bleistein, jumped every fence and ditch that came their way.

In a closet in his den, the president kept an assortment of swords and staffs for himself and his guests. They practiced their skills at fencing and single stick (fighting with poles). Frequently the president took part in boxing matches with visitors until a young captain unknowingly hit the president's left eye so hard it blinded him. Roosevelt kept that a secret.

The president then turned to ju-jitsu, welcoming Japanese masters to teach him this exotic sport. Roosevelt proudly showed off his new skills by "throwing" a Swiss diplomat who was visiting the White House.

Archie, Quentin, Theodore, Edith, and Ted Roosevelt on horseback at Sagamore Hill. The horses traveled with the family to the White House. Algonquin, the calico pony, made an appearance in the White House elevator.

Sagamore Hill National Historical Site, National Park Service

7

The President Goes Global

ONCE HE made his name as a trust buster, Theodore Roosevelt began to flex his muscles in world affairs. The president looked at countries on the map as though he were viewing a chessboard. International events set a worldwide stage for the big game of diplomacy that went on among Germany, Great Britain, Russia, and Japan. All had colonies in Africa and Asia. Each needed to keep order—with a navy to assist them.

The United States had never embarked on a great quest to build colonies in Africa or Asia, but when Theodore Roosevelt came to the office of president in 1901, it was a different world. The United States was not a young republic trying to build itself from scratch into a modern nation. The country had expanded "from sea to shining sea" and held territories around the world.

Ever the realist, Roosevelt sensed that the United States was destined to become another mighty player in foreign affairs, starting with the Western Hemisphere. Roosevelt believed in America's duty to defend the Western Hemisphere from European powers.

He had reason to worry. In the early 1900s, governments in Central America and the Caribbean were far from stable. Many had loans from Europe that they did not pay back. From time to time, Germany and Italy sent warships to Latin America to settle disputes.

Roosevelt did not want Europeans to meddle in the Americas. Again, he relied on the Monroe Doctrine as his weapon of choice. In 1904, Roosevelt issued his warning: If any country in Central America or the Caribbean misbehaved, the United States would deal with the problem. Europe must stay out.

OPPOSITE: The First Family posed on the lawn at Sagamore Hill. Left to right: Quentin, Theodore, Ted, Archie, Alice, Kermit, Edith, and Ethel.
Library of Congress LC-USZ62-113665

The president's declaration took his name to become the Roosevelt Corollary to the Monroe Doctrine. (A corollary is an add-on.)

Problems on the Pacific

ROOSEVELT HAD other concerns. Ever since he was assistant secretary of the navy, the Russian and Japanese empires had grown stronger. The Russian and Japanese navies also posed a threat to American trade in China, Hawaii, and the Philippines.

The new president inherited a small but bloody war in the Philippines. The war had started while Roosevelt was still governor of New York.

After Dewey's fleet crushed Spanish rule in the island colony in 1898, the United States decided that the Filipino people were too "primitive" to govern themselves. Conveniently, the island also provided a perfect location to fuel and supply navy ships as they sailed the Pacific Ocean. The Philippines lured American businessmen with raw materials to supply their factories and promised ready markets for the goods they manufactured.

However, the Filipinos rose in revolt to demand their independence from the United States. Savage fighting followed as both American and Filipino fighters broke the rules of war and tortured their prisoners.

In the United States, opinions split about whether the Philippines should be granted independence. On one side stood the anti-imperialists, including William Jennings Bryan and the author Mark Twain. Anti-imperialists argued that the United States had no business trying to create colonies and build empires.

On the other side stood President McKinley, Secretary of State John Hay, and Secretary of War Elihu Root. Roosevelt, then governor of New York, agreed.

When Roosevelt ran for vice president in 1900, he accused Bryan of being two-faced. Bryan, Roosevelt charged, was calling for Filipino independence—while ignoring the sorry fact that African Americans in the South could not vote. The Filipino people, Roosevelt said, needed America's protection until they earned their independence. America "should train them for self government as rapidly as possible and then leave them free to decide their own fate."

After President McKinley died, Roosevelt kept Hay and Root at their posts. Unlike McKinley, Roosevelt himself devised foreign policy at his desk in the White House. Then he directed Hay and Root to carry it out.

The president talked about how to "walk softly and carry a big stick." But he knew how to use a sword, as well. Roosevelt went

Life magazine poked fun by drawing Theodore Roosevelt as a map of North and Central America.

at his job as the nation's commander in chief like a swordsman taking aim at his foe.

Roosevelt championed America's growth as a world power.

The policy of expansion is America's historic policy. We have annexed the Philippines exactly as we have annexed Hawaii, New Mexico, and Alaska. They are now part of the American territory and we have no more right to give them up than we have the right to restore Hawaii to the [former] Kanaka Queen or to abandon Alaska to the Esquimaux [Eskimos].

The champion of America's global interests still believed in sea power. In a day when airplanes were still a dream, Roosevelt called for a U.S. Navy rivaled by no one. Then he persuaded Congress to give him the funds to build it. By the end of Roosevelt's second term in office in 1907, the American fleet boasted 20 battleships, standing second only to Great Britain's Royal Navy.

To celebrate, the president ordered 26 navy vessels to be painted white and sail around the world. This Great White Fleet was supposed to signal America's peaceful intentions, but Roosevelt's message was clear. Germany and Japan could see the might of American sea power. Both, however, failed to remember Roosevelt's lesson. Later in the 1900s, Germany and Japan declared war on the United States. The U.S. Navy helped to defeat them both.

In 1905 *Puck* magazine showed "Columbia," a symbol of the United States, dressed in armor, on the bow of a battleship with Theodore Roosevelt's face on it. Library of Congress LC-USZC4-2624

PLAY SIPA

WHEN THE United States Navy docked in the Philippine Islands, sailors watched children play *sipa*, which means "kick" in Tagalog, one of the Filipino languages spoken in Manila. They used their feet and shins to keep a small washer called a sipa in the air. Each sipa was decorated with colorful string. This game resembled hacky sack, a game that the sailors played with a small pouch stuffed with beans.

You can make your own sipa and play a game.

You'll Need

- Colored yarn or strips of colored plastic
- Scissors
- Ruler
- Metal washer about the size of a quarter
- Two or more players

Measure 5 or 6 pieces of yarn and cut them into 1-foot lengths, or cut 6 strips from plastic bags about ¾ inch wide and 12 inches long.

Tie the ends of the strings or strips of plastic to the washer and secure them with a small knot.

You will need to practice with your sipa before you start the game. The rules say that you must use only part of your foot, ankle, or leg below your knee to keep the sipa in the air. If it hits the ground, you're out!

Practice until you can kick your sipa high. Your best kicks can take your sipa above your head. When everyone feels comfortable kicking the sipa, decide on the number of kicks a player must make in order to win a round.

Choose who goes first by playing another Filipino tradition: *jack-en-poy*. This is simply rock, paper, scissors.

The loser becomes "It" and starts the game by tossing the sipa gently into the air. The other player must catch the sipa with his or her foot and keep the sipa airborne for the agreed-upon number of kicks. If the sipa falls to the ground before then, the kicker becomes "It." However, if the player reaches the required number of kicks, then he or she kicks the sipa so that the "It" player can catch it with his or her foot and get a turn.

You might want to try a newer version of sipa and use your feet, legs, palms of your hands, arms, and elbows.

Obviously, the player who keeps the sipa airborne the longest is the winner. However, you might want to pair up and play sipa as teams, and pass the sipa back and forth between turns without ever letting it land on the ground.

A Man, a Plan, a Canal—Panama!

ANTI-IMPERIALISTS ALSO squawked when President Roosevelt waved his big stick at Panama in Central America, calling for a canal to be built there. The navy was wasting precious time, taking days to sail down the east coast of South America and cross through the Strait of Magellan into the Pacific.

One look at a map showed it made perfect sense to dig a canal through the isthmus, a narrow thread of land in Panama. A French company was planning to do exactly that, but there was a problem. Tiny Panama was an unwilling "state" of neighboring Colombia, which was willing to sell land for a canal—but at an outrageous price. A way out, Roosevelt knew, would be for Panamanians to declare independence from Colombia and sell the land themselves.

On the scene there appeared one of the era's most colorful characters, Philippe Bunau-Varilla, a handsome French engineer who worked for the canal company. Thousands of miles from Panama, Bunau-Varilla set up headquarters in the Waldorf-Astoria Hotel in New York. There, he and a group of friends engineered a revolution in Panama. Mrs. Bunau-Varilla even designed and sewed a flag for the new country.

On the night of November 3, 1903, as a U.S. Navy cruiser stood offshore, a small band of firemen, railroad workers, and Colombian army deserters staged a revolution in Panama. By the next day, U.S. troops were on hand as Panama declared its independence. Mrs. Bunau-Varilla's flag was raised, and Bunau-Varilla made himself a diplomat of the new nation. He entered into a treaty with Roosevelt that gave the United States the Panama Canal Zone, a strip of land across Panama 10 miles wide.

As president, Roosevelt could make a treaty, but only the United States Senate could ratify one. The anti-imperialists in the Senate shouted protests at Roosevelt's handling of the affair. In the end, they lost by a vote of 66 to 14.

The United States paid the French company $40 million for its assets and the work already started. Colombia did not get a single dime—until years later, when President Woodrow Wilson suggested that it was time to make amends and pay Colombia $25 million. That was an "act of infamy" in Roosevelt's eyes. To pay Colombia anything made the United States look like a partner in Panama's revolution. Roosevelt disputed any notion "that this nation has played the part of a thief." Even so, the past president would be known to brag that he had "taken the Isthmus."

A magazine cover crowned Theodore Roosevelt for his "greatest achievement for trade in modern times."
Library of Congress LC-USZ62-75561

81

PALINDROMES

THEODORE ROOSEVELT successfully pushed his plan to build a waterway across Central America. Someone who liked to play with words came up with a slogan to honor the president:

A Man, a Plan, a Canal—Panama!

What do you notice about the slogan?

The sentence reads the same right to left as it does left to right.

Sentences like this are called palindromes. These have appeared in languages from Greek and Latin to Russian and Japanese. Often they are funny, such as this sign you might see in a vet's office:

STEP ON NO PETS.

Incidentally, the word meaning a female sheep is also a palindrome. Can you guess it?

ewe

Can you write a palindrome? Here's a hint. Think about words that read forward and backward exactly the same. You also can try stringing short words together to create a palindrome.

After you've written a few, enjoy these famous palindromes:

MA SAW A HAM.

MADAM, I'M ADAM.

A DOG! A PANIC IN A PAGODA!

WAS IT A CAR OR A CAT I SAW?

DO GEESE SEE GOD?

EVA, CAN I SEE BEES IN A CAVE?

YO, BANANA BOY!

In the summer of 1904, the United States began to dig across Panama. Theodore Roosevelt had waved his big stick and won his canal.

Entertaining with Grace and Style

As the wife of an important man, Edith Roosevelt served as hostess to friends and people in government. There was always room for guests at their table, but paying for them worried her. When Theodore became vice president in 1901, he had to host guests at his own expense. He earned an $8,000 salary, much less than as governor of New York.

The family's finances brightened when the Roosevelts moved into the White House. With the president's salary of $50,000 per year plus an allowance, Edith could entertain with the style and grace of a First Lady. She hosted evening musicales that brought noted performers to the White House. One young performer was an up-and-coming cellist named Pablo Casals; he came again 60 years later as a guest of the Kennedys.

Edith also oversaw Alice's debut into society at a White House party. Alice was miffed that Edith would not pay for a fancy ball with champagne and pricey favors such as silver

Edith Roosevelt joined her husband to greet visitors to the White House every New Year's Day. Edith held flowers so that she would not have to shake hands with every guest, as Theodore did. Library of Congress LC-USZ62-127062

Edith Roosevelt established a portrait gallery of America's first ladies in the White House. Library of Congress LC-USZ62-12a

cigarette cases and fur-trimmed muffs. Nonetheless, Alice's Aunt Corinne reported that Alice looked happy as young men swarmed around her.

Edith ordered new china to replace worn pieces of White House dishes that had seen better days. In order to accomplish her goals, she hired a social secretary, a first for a president's wife. Edith, noted the White House usher, was a favorite of the servants working there.

Edith Roosevelt, living in the White House at the turn of the 20th century, set the tone for the role of First Lady in modern times.

A Roosevelt Christmas

Winter brought cold-weather fun to Sagamore Hill—sledding, sleighing on an old wagon attached to runners, and a sport new to Americans using Norwegian snowshoes, or skis! Of course, Christmas was a special time.

On Christmas Eve, the family journeyed to the Episcopal Church in Oyster Bay for services. For years Theodore, the church's leading citizen, offered the Christmas Eve message. Then it was back up the hill for Christmas itself. Christmas Day was for the children, who opened stockings in their parents' bedroom. Then, snug in their robes and Theodore in his brocade "wrapper," everyone climbed the stairs to the frosty gunroom where their Christmas tree and big presents awaited them.

When the Roosevelts lived in the White House, they spent Christmas there. The day after Christmas 1905, President Roosevelt wrote about his holiday to a young friend.

Jimmikens:

... Yesterday morning at a quarter of seven all the children were up and dressed and began to hammer at the door of their mother's and my room, in which their six stockings, all bulging out with queer angles and rotundities, were hanging from the fireplace. So their mother and I got up, shut the window, lit the fire, taking down the stockings, of course, put on our wrappers and prepared to admit the children. But first there was a surprise for me, also for their good mother, for Archie had a little Christmas tree of his own which he had rigged up with the help of one of

the carpenters in a big closet; and we all had to look at the tree and each of us got a present off of it. There was also one present each for Jack the dog, Tom Quartz the kitten, and Algonquin the pony.... Then all the children came into our bed and there they opened their stockings. Afterwards we got dressed and took breakfast and then all went into the library, where each child had a table set for his bigger presents. Quentin had a perfectly delightful electric railroad, which had been rigged up for him by one of his friends, the White House electrician, who has been very good to all the children.

The president went on to report that he went for a three-hour horseback ride, had lunch, and played a game of single stick with his friends.

We have to try to hit as light as possible, but sometimes we hit hard, and to-day I have a bump over one eye and a swollen wrist. Then all our family and kinsfolk and Senator and Mrs. Lodge's family and kinsfolk had our Christmas dinner at the White House, and afterwards danced in the East Room, closing up with the Virginia Reel.

For years, stories about this Christmas appeared. They said that President Roosevelt—a strict conservationist—had outlawed Christmas trees in the White House, and that Archie had sneaked one in. Recently, however, historians have debunked that story. There is no evidence that the president ever outlawed Christmas trees.

The President Turns Progressive

MARCH 4, 1905, opened with a whoop and a holler as a band of Rough Riders clattered down Washington's streets. The horsemen had come to herald the inauguration of Theodore Roosevelt as he returned for a full term as president. A few hapless citizens even found themselves roped by visiting cowboys in town to celebrate.

The party carried on all day as bands marched and crowds cheered to the tune "There'll Be a Hot Time in the Old Town Tonight." Roosevelt beamed. Now he was president, he said, all "in my own right."

Rightly proud, Roosevelt had fought to win Republican backing for his nomination the summer before. Republican Party bosses liked other candidates who were not busy busting trusts. However, the party could see

ABOVE: A group of Native American chiefs rode in Theodore Roosevelt's inaugural parade in 1905. The one wearing a hat is Geronimo, a famed Apache chief. Library of Congress LC-USZ62-56009 **BELOW:** Soldiers and onlookers crowded the East Portico of the Capitol for the Roosevelt inauguration in 1905. Library of Congress LC-DIG-ppmsca-19619

the president's popular stand with ordinary Americans and gave Roosevelt the nod. In the November election, he handily defeated Judge Alton B. Parker, the Democrats' candidate.

Roosevelt didn't know that money from big corporations, including a monumental sum of $125,000 from the Standard Oil Company, helped him win the White House. Still, it turned out that the business tycoons in the Republican Party made a bad bet. Roosevelt was turning toward a progressive outlook that grew ever clearer.

A political cartoon showed Standard Oil as a giant octopus with tentacles reaching into industries, state legislatures, and the U.S. Capitol, and toward the White House. Library of Congress LC-USZ62-26205

Square of body and square of face, Theodore Roosevelt had promised Americans a "square deal" when he made a speech at the Grand Canyon in 1903. He had vowed to balance the interests of businesspeople on one side and working people on the other—fair and square. Theodore Roosevelt now knew how to use the power of the presidency to make reform actually happen.

He began by urging Congress to pass a law. Roosevelt planned to change the way railway companies fixed prices for hauling freight across state lines in interstate commerce. Of all America's businesses, the nation's network of railroads was the biggest. Typically, railroads charged lower fees to special customers. Giant companies such as Standard Oil enjoyed special prices. Small-business owners and farmers were fed up with the high rates they paid to ship their products.

The system wasn't fair, the president claimed. Railway owners should not play favorites with one company over another, nor gouge private passengers either. But the president had a fight on his hands when he asked Congress to pass the bill, known as the Hepburn Act. It went further than any law by handing control of the railroads to the U.S. Interstate Commerce Commission. The House of Representatives passed the bill easily. They had heard all the complaints.

But in the Senate, matters were different. In 1906 senators were elected not by the people in their states but by state legislatures more tuned in to big business. When it came time to vote on the reform bill, "railroad men" in the Senate cried foul.

Theodore Roosevelt went to the people, making speech after speech across the country to push his ideas for reform. Though change was in the air, Roosevelt finally had to tweak the bill to please the holdouts in the Senate. His game plan of "give a little, take a lot" worked, and the Senate passed the law.

Roosevelt then focused on another abuse of the public trust. When he came into office, the government had little official concern for the health of its citizens. But America was on the move, changing from a nation of famers to a nation of city dwellers.

Americans were fast becoming consumers who shopped in markets. No one could be sure that the food on his or her table was safe. People no longer grew their own vegetables or butchered their own meat. Moreover, housewives bought medicines from "snake oil salesmen" who hawked products door-to-door. Many times, these medications were little more than liquor, heroin, or cocaine.

On occasion, companies regulated themselves. For example, meatpackers, looking for better profits, sometimes asked inspectors to certify that their products were safe. But such self-policing rarely took place. More often, the beef trust took advantage of naive consumers, doing their dirty work with not a worry about Americans' health.

But a growing middle class, Americans who read newspapers and books, began to ask for better. And when they read a bestselling book about a meatpacking plant, change came in a hurry.

Young boys worked stuffing sausages at a Chicago meatpacking plant.
Library of Congress LC-USZ62-97452

Enshrined and Enshrouded: The Brownsville Affair

In the summer of 1906, three companies of African American soldiers, members of the 25th Infantry, Colored, were posted to Fort Brown in Brownsville, Texas. Brownsville was a segregated town. Its white citizens looked disgusted when black soldiers walked on their streets. Tensions grew. The Brownsville newspaper reported that a black soldier had attacked a white woman. On the night of August 13, the 25th's officers ordered the men confined to post to avoid trouble.

Nonetheless, late that evening, a mob of unidentified men shot up homes and saloons in Brownsville. The mob killed a bartender and wounded a policeman. In the fort, officers quickly called the soldiers to line up for roll call and inspected their weapons. Not one soldier was missing; no weapons had been fired.

As Commander in Chief of the Army, President Roosevelt called for an investigation. Townspeople claimed they had seen black soldiers fire their Springfield rifles and produced empty shells to prove it. Army investigators could not find a single soldier to admit to the shooting. One thought the entire group had agreed together to stay silent but stated that there was "no evidence" of it.

In 1906 no official would publicly accuse white townspeople in Brownsville of dressing like soldiers and shooting up the place themselves.

To keep black votes for Republicans, Roosevelt waited until after the mid-term election of 1906. Then he gave his decision: every man in the 25th Infantry was to be dishonorably discharged from the army. The president claimed that the black soldiers should have turned over the guilty ones for punishment.

Not one would receive a pension to see him through old age. Although the 25th included six Medal of Honor winners and soldiers who had fought with Roosevelt in Cuba, everyone received the same harsh punishment. Not one was allowed a trial.

Then the president dropped the matter and left the country to inspect the building of the Panama Canal. It was the first time any U.S. president had traveled beyond the nation's shores. The president was ready to glory in his achievement.

At home, Roosevelt's political opponents spoke out against his decision. But the protests were not sincere. Many in Congress simply used the Brownsville soldiers as a convenient excuse to attack the president. So Roosevelt dug in his heels and stood by his order.

In time, Roosevelt backed off, and 14 of the dishonored soldiers were allowed to re-enlist. But the damage was done. Booker T. Washington spoke of his dismay to the president. Louder criticism came from W. E. B. DuBois, a young African American calling for change *now* for blacks. Roosevelt was "once enshrined in our love as our Moses," roared a black pastor, but now the president was "enshrouded in our scorn as our Judas."

No one ever pinpointed who shot up Brownsville in 1906. Roosevelt's personal assistant, an African American named James Amos, insisted later that some Brownsville soldiers had confessed their guilt in person to the president.

In 1970 a historian dug into the case. Then the army, which no longer punished an entire unit for the actions of a few, acted to make things right.

A search for survivors of the 25th Infantry turned up just one, a man named Dorsie Willis who worked shining shoes. Sixty years after the injustice, he received an honorable discharge from the army and $25,000 for a lifetime lived under a cloud of shame.

In February 1906 a writer named Upton Sinclair published *The Jungle*. A political novel, the book told of dirt-poor immigrants who labored in Chicago's slaughterhouses. Sinclair disguised himself as a meatpacker to see working conditions for himself. His brutal images of filth in the plants turned his readers' stomachs. In *The Jungle*, Sinclair wrote about missing workers who fell into giant vats and "all but the bones of them had gone out to the world as Durham's Pure Leaf Lard." (Lard is fat used to fry food.)

The outcry was so loud Theodore Roosevelt secretly sent inspectors to see for themselves. Could packing plants possibly be as dreadful as Sinclair said?

Roosevelt's inspectors reported back.

We saw meat shoveled from filthy wooden floors, piled on tables rarely washed, pushed from room to room in rotten box carts, in all of which processes it was in the way of gathering dirt, splinters, floor filth, and the expectoration [spit] of tuberculosis and other diseased workers.

The Jungle caused such a stir Congress quickly passed the Pure Food and Drug and Meat Inspection Acts. Now the federal government was to take charge of the public safety. However, the president warned Americans, while "muckrakers" such as Sinclair served their purpose, they must not sensationalize their stories. Roosevelt had no use for yellow journalism. Be "absolutely truthful," Roosevelt warned. The president wanted public discussion to stay in balance.

Theodore Roosevelt's Grand Plan

SINCE THE days of the Pilgrims and pioneers, Americans had reveled in all the opportunities the land offered. Few gave any thought to the rights of the people who had lived there for centuries. Americans hungered for land and its natural resources—wood from forests, coal and ore from mines, grasslands for ranchers, and fertile soils for farmers. All stood ripe for Americans to use—and to use up.

For 50 years before Roosevelt's presidency, Americans had worked the land with little thought about how to care for it. Half of the country's native forests were clear-cut—and gone. Sheep had grazed acres of western lands bare of grass, and erosion set in. Crude farming methods added to the problem as soil washed away. Buffalo, once so thick they looked like a vast brown blanket rippling across the plains, were nearly extinct. Fashionable women wore dead birds as decorations on their hats, as colonies of

Bodies of birds adorned women's hats in the late 1800s and early 1900s. Library of Congress LC-USZ62-61248

white-feathered pelicans and snowy egrets were nearly hunted out.

President Roosevelt thrilled to the chase of hunting big game—including buffalo. Yet Roosevelt recognized the threat to America's natural resources. Roosevelt and his fellow hunters, who understood the delicate balance of life in the great outdoors, were among the first to call for conservation. They joined forces with naturalists such as John Muir, John Burroughs, and Frank Chapman to protect the land and defend its birds and animals.

The president began his program to urge Congress to pass the Newlands Act in 1902, which set up a plan for bringing water to three million acres of dry western land. Engineers designed huge dams to hold river water in reservoirs. At planting time, water flowed from the reservoirs through irrigation ditches, and the land grew rich with crops.

Then Roosevelt followed up on the pleas of Chapman, a bird scientist, to protect snowy egrets living on Pelican Island, government land in Florida. Roosevelt used his executive power as president to declare the tiny island a Federal Wildlife Refuge. Pelican Island was but the first of 51 bird preserves that Roosevelt named across the United States and its territories of Alaska and Hawaii.

At the same time, the president launched a movement to protect the buffalo. Lands in Kansas, the Grand Canyon, Alaska, and Montana found their way into national game preserves to shield animals as diverse as buffalo and sea lions from the guns of hunters.

In 1905, Roosevelt appointed his friend Gifford Pinchot to lead the newly formed U.S. Forest Service. Pinchot aimed to add thousands of acres of timberland to the reserves already held by the government. However, many Westerners objected because they felt they knew better how to deal with their own land than any Easterner ever could. Two years later, their men in Congress tacked on a rider to a farming bill that the president knew he must sign. The rider would yank power from the president to create more land reserves and place it solely in the hands of Congress.

But Theodore Roosevelt, who knew a thing or two about the game of politics, outplayed his opponents in Congress. Roosevelt and Pinchot already had a plan in place. Just two days before he had to sign the farm bill, Theodore Roosevelt signed an executive order to add 16 million acres of land to the nation's reserves. In his *Autobiography*, Roosevelt explained how he hoodwinked his opponents.

[W]hen the friends of the special interests in the Senate got their amendment through and woke up, they discovered

Theodore Roosevelt posed with John Muir, a conservationist, on Glacier Point in the Yosemite Valley, California. Library of Congress LC-USZC4-4698

USE SUNSHINE TO DRAW A PICTURE

BRIGHT DAYS outdoors are the perfect time to experiment with one of Teedie Roosevelt's favorite tools: the magnifying glass. You can use one to capture the sun's rays and burn an image on a piece of wood. Years ago, this hobby was simply called woodburning.

Today there are artists who make a living at wood burning, or writing with fire, but they've updated the name of their art and now call it solar pyrography. With a bit of practice, you can write with fire as well.

Adult supervision required

You'll Need

❖ Sunny day
❖ Pail of water
❖ Strong sunglasses
❖ Large magnifying glass
❖ Pieces of firewood or old boards
❖ Pencil

Find a place outside, in the sun, where you can work undisturbed. Make sure to have a pail of water nearby just in case. Put on a pair of sunglasses. Sit with the sun behind you. Depending on the season and time of day, the sun will be high or low in the sky—maybe almost overhead.

Hold a magnifying glass between the sun and your wood, then move it back and forth until it makes a bright point of light on the wood. In just seconds, the wood should begin to smoke, and then a small tongue of flame should appear. The wood will start to burn.

Now move your hand and arm slowly as you direct the point of light across the wood. Keep the spot of sunshine as small as possible. As you move your hand, the sunlight will follow your motion and burn a pattern. Practice making straight lines, curves, and circles. Try writing your name. Then see if you can "draw" a simple image.

When you think you have practiced enough, use a pencil to lightly trace a design on a good log or piece of wood. Then burn the image with the magnifying glass. Work slowly and carefully, and you'll have a piece of art to be proud of!

Roosevelt's Game of Football

When Theodore and Edith's young son Ted left for boarding school at Groton, he seemed homesick at first. But as he settled into his new school, Ted sent letters with happy news about dormitory football and other adventures.

Theodore and Edith wrote regular letters to catch Ted up on the antics at home. Theodore filled his with advice to his son about choices he made. As Ted read them, he could hear his father's voice.

I am delighted to have you play football. I believe in rough, manly sports.... I don't want you to sacrifice standing well in your studies to any over-athleticism; and I need not tell you that character counts for a great deal more than either intellect or body in winning success in life. Athletic proficiency is a mighty good servant, and like many other good servants, a mighty bad master.

Theodore Roosevelt played football with his children at Sagamore Hill. Sagamore Hill National Historic Site, National Park Service

However, football was dangerous. In 1905 alone, 18 players died, including three college students. They had little in the way of protective helmets and pads. One risky play was Harvard's flying wedge mass formation, when blockers locked arms and the defense tried to break though. President Roosevelt called in representatives from Harvard, Yale, and Princeton for a meeting. In the White House, the group decided that the game of football needed a new set of rules to protect its players.

Out of that meeting came the modern game of football, complete with new rules against mass plays (where the offense aimed all of its players against one man on the defensive line). The new rules also established a neutral zone between teams before the start of each play.

For the first time, the rules of football allowed the forward pass. This move, now legal, changed the game forever as it "opened up" play on the field.

that sixteen million acres of timberland had been saved for the people by putting them in the National Forests before the land grabbers could get at them.

The opponents of the Forest Service turned handsprings in their wrath...

As the president worked to preserve the country's forests, he also set his sights on America's historic monuments. Souvenir hunters were running wild across prehistoric Indian home sites and burial grounds digging for treasured artifacts. Roosevelt talked Congress into passing the Antiquities Act. The law gave the president executive power to preserve landmarks, prehistoric sites, and "other objects of historic or scientific interest."

Roosevelt's actions to take charge of historic and cultural sites came not a moment too soon. He had heard the talk. Land developers had big plans to "improve" the majestic Grand Canyon with a string of tourist hotels along its scenic South Rim. But Congress refused to preserve the Grand Canyon as a national park.

Fine, said President Roosevelt. The solution was simple. Again, he played politics. This time, he used his executive authority to declare the Grand Canyon a national monument—all 1,250 square miles of it. After all, Roosevelt winked, who could deny that the Grand Canyon was a point of "scientific interest"?

The president strode far ahead of most Americans in his quest to save the nation's natural beauty from destruction. Over the course of seven years, Theodore Roosevelt set aside 18 national monuments, 150 national forests, and 5 national parks. In 1916, after he left office, he saw his actions give birth to the U.S. National Park Service, a federal agency to manage the treasures held in trust for all Americans.

Theodore Roosevelt used his power as president to preserve the Grand Canyon for all Americans.
Library of Congress Geography and Map Division

President Roosevelt's able—and awesome—use of executive power gave Americans his greatest gift.

The President Scores a Victory

IN ADDITION to making reforms on the home front, President Roosevelt dealt with international problems during his second term. He worried about the growing threat that Germany's mighty army presented to the rest of Europe and the Middle East. Since Germany's varied regions had become unified under one flag in the 1880s, its kaiser, Wilhelm II, had built his proud nation into a military giant.

There were other regions that weighed on the president's mind, too. Early in 1904 the Japanese Navy attacked the Russian fleet at Port Arthur, Manchuria, a part of China. Both the Japanese and Russian empires had pushed into new territories in Asia, and Japan felt that Russia had moved too far. Their aggression also threatened the United States's Open Door policy—a plan to ensure

Theodore Roosevelt warns Nicholas II to stop Russia's persecution of Jews in this 1905 illustration.
Library of Congress LC-DIG-ppmsca-05438

equal access to China for American business and political interests.

Quietly, Roosevelt supported Japan. Russia's emperor, the czar, and his ruling class did nothing to build a strong middle class in Russia, and its peasants starved. Further, Russia's elite looked the other way when mobs attacked Jewish villagers in vicious pogroms, or organized massacres. But as Japan kept winning battles over the next year, the president became concerned about the balance of power in Asia. He did not want to see Japan grow too strong and threaten American interests.

In August 1905 Roosevelt called for a conference in Portsmouth, New Hampshire, where both sides could find a way to end the war. Although the president didn't take part in face-to-face talks between the Japanese and Russians, his outsized personality loomed over them. Behind the scenes, Roosevelt wrote to anyone who could influence either side. He sought the help of British diplomats. Even though he did not trust Germany's Kaiser Wilhelm, he asked him to talk sense to the Russian czar, Nicholas II, who was Wilhelm's cousin.

"I am having my hair turned gray," he wrote to his son Kermit. "The Japanese ask too much, but the Russians are 10 times worse than the Japs because they are so stupid and won't tell the truth."

When it looked as though the enemies could not reach a solution over disputed land and claims about money, the president suggested a compromise. Surprisingly, it worked. The savage Russo-Japanese War came to an end.

The next year, the president received news from Christiania, Norway (now its capital, Oslo). The Norwegian government had awarded him the world's most notable honor, the Nobel Peace Prize, for bringing an end to the war.

"The Portsmouth Drama." Theodore Roosevelt is flanked by the czar of Russia and the emperor of Japan in this 1905 postcard. Below them are diplomats from Russia and Japan.
Library of Congress LC-USZ62-78462

End of an Era

As THEODORE Roosevelt moved toward the end of his second term as president, he grew bolder. By now a true progressive, Roosevelt used his position as chief executive to clamor even louder for reform.

President Roosevelt still went after businesses that abused his notion of the Square Deal for ordinary Americans. He asked the Department of Commerce and Labor to investigate cases of children who worked at adult jobs. He pushed for an eight-hour work day for everyone. He continued to press for

"Don't be afraid Uncle.—We'll get there all right!"

Copyrighted 1907. by
Fred C. Lounsbury.

ABOVE: A postcard of President Roosevelt pictures him as a race car driver with a terrified Uncle Sam riding along.
RIGHT: A poster calls out factory owners who hired children to work instead of encouraging them to go to school.
Library of Congress LC-DIG-nclc-04928

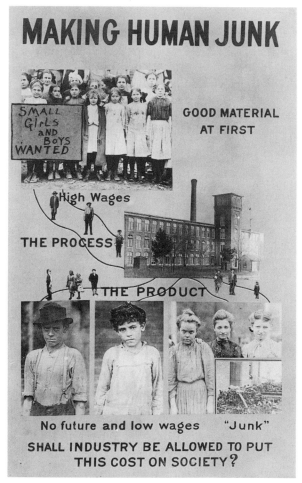

MAKING HUMAN JUNK

SMALL GIRLS AND BOYS WANTED

GOOD MATERIAL AT FIRST

High Wages

THE PROCESS

THE PRODUCT

No future and low wages   "Junk"

SHALL INDUSTRY BE ALLOWED TO PUT THIS COST ON SOCIETY?

96

The White House Gang

By the time Quentin got to school, Roosevelts were familiar faces in class. However, when the youngest Roosevelt entered the Force Public School in Washington, tongues wagged. Quentin was quick and smart—and a holy terror. He made friends with a group of six other boys, soon nicknamed the White House Gang. ("Gang" meant simply a group of kids in those days.) They ran the streets as many kids did, playing games and sometimes getting in trouble.

The White House Gang was welcome at Quentin's home. On occasion, Quentin's father called the boys to task—the first time when they decorated a painting of President Andrew Jackson with spitballs stuck on the portrait's ears, forehead, buttons, and nose. Another day, Theodore ran full force into a post chasing them through the attic. Charlie Taft (son of the next president) had switched off the light.

After the gang grew up, another member recalled another event. On a snowy afternoon, the boys ran upstairs and rolled a giant snowball off the White House portico (a covered walkway) directly onto a policeman. The president was just coming outdoors to meet his carriage. "The horses jumped and lunged. The coachman stood up, and pulling on his reins with all his strength, held them in. The footman ... clutched at TR [Roosevelt]."

The president looked up at the portico and shook his fist at Quentin. He roundly scolded the boys, "[F]ortunately for you, you haven't broken his neck." Just as bad, Roosevelt explained, they had robbed the policeman of his dignity in front of the president. "Think of his feelings! He saw that I saw the whole business, from beginning to end. He saw, even that I laughed. I should not have done so, of course, but how could I help it? It *made* me laugh! It was *terrible*!"

His orders followed: "[Y]ou will tender him an apology, not perfunctorily offered, but handsomely, and in real sincerity." Roosevelt spoke like a president to the boys, and they obeyed him to the letter.

Archie and Quentin Roosevelt joined a roll call of Washington D.C. policemen.
Library of Congress LC–USZ62–83135

the government to make stronger rules controlling railroad prices.

Roosevelt floated the idea of a graduated income tax for all Americans to pay based on how much they earned. The president also believed that the rich should pay taxes on wealth that they inherited from family members.

Roosevelt's opponents in Congress railed against the president's plans to expand the power of the federal government. However,

IN 1909 Theodore Roosevelt hand-picked a sculptor named Victor David Brenner to design the first Lincoln penny. The president wanted to honor his hero, and he admired an image of Lincoln that Brenner had sculpted.

The Lincoln penny's 100-year history has seen several changes to its design and metallic composition. During World War II, when copper was scarce, the U.S. Mint made steel pennies in 1943. In 1958 the back of the penny changed from its "wheat" design to an image of the Lincoln Memorial. Some pennies were minted in Denver with a "D" next to the date; others, in San Francisco (look for the tiny "S").

You can collect Lincoln pennies and display them. Some, such as the 1943 steel penny, are hard to find. But you can easily start by collecting pennies minted in the last 20 or 30 years.

Adult supervision required

You'll Need
❖ Penny
❖ Ruler
❖ Pencil
❖ A styrofoam block about the size of a brick (preferably one you rescue from the trash)
❖ Small sharp knife

Measure the penny at its widest point. Write down this measurement.

Use the ruler to draw a series of light, parallel lines across the foam block. Space them at least two inches apart. The number of lines you draw depends on how large your penny collection will be.

Now use the knife to cut a series of slits along the lines. The slits should be the same size as your penny.

Where should you look for pennies for your collection? Look through your change when you go to the store. Lots of families have pennies stuffed in jars. And check with older family members; many older people have squirreled away pennies from their childhood. See if you can find at least one for each year.

When you find pennies for your collection, insert them into the foam block. Leave space for the missing ones. As your collection grows, you can add a second block.

This 1943 steel penny has started to rust.

Theodore Roosevelt was the subject of writers, musicians, artists, and sculptors. Salvator Erseny Florio sculpted Roosevelt for a South American museum.

the president kept on pushing for change. He warned that if reforms did not come, then American workers would be drawn to what he called the dangerous ideas of socialists such as Eugene Debs.

Debs made his name as a labor leader during a strike by workers against the Pullman Palace Car Company, which made railroad sleeper cars in Chicago. As a socialist, Debs believed that the government—not private citizens—should run businesses and the economy.

Roosevelt wanted another term in the White House, but he couldn't run for it. During his acceptance speech in the election back in 1904, the president had made the biggest political mistake of his career. Caught up in the emotion of that evening, the president had promised—in the spirit of George Washington—not to run for a third term. (Edith Roosevelt's quick frown when he made his promise that night showed he had made a mistake.)

Because he felt he could not run again, Roosevelt turned to a candidate whom he saw as a safe bet: William Howard Taft, his secretary of war. The easygoing and bright Taft seemed to agree with the president's reform-minded ways. The Republicans nominated Taft at their convention, although a wild floor demonstration by Roosevelt fans proved how popular the president still was. Taft defeated

Near the end of his second term, Theodore and Edith traveled to Panama to inspect construction of the canal. It was the first time a U.S. president left American shores. Library of Congress

the Democrats' man, William Jennings Bryan, in the presidential election of 1908.

In March 1909 Theodore Roosevelt bade farewell to the White House. Already he had an uneasy feeling that Taft would not follow his path toward reform. The weather seemed to agree. It had been a cold, bright day when Roosevelt took the inaugural oath in 1905. When it became Taft's turn four years later, he took it in the middle of a snowstorm.

8

Roosevelt the Adventurer

THEODORE ROOSEVELT was only 50 years old when he left the White House. He felt restless and full of energy. After taking charge of the nation, Roosevelt needed a new challenge. He found one in Africa, a continent that was still little understood in the early 1900s. Taking 19-year-old Kermit along for company, the former president sailed for Africa to embark on a months-long safari. Roosevelt's safari began in Mombassa on the Indian Ocean and wound through British East Africa. Then the Roosevelt party worked its way north across the Sudan to Cairo, Egypt.

"Safari" means "journey" in the African language of Swahili. Roosevelt's safari lasted nine months and turned out to be more of an expedition than a simple journey. As rough as the land was, the trek offered many of the comforts of home. Hundreds of local people were hired to come along with the hunting party as porters, guides, cooks, and guards.

Roosevelt took along a portable tub for his daily hot bath and a collection of books bound in pigskin to protect them against oil and dust. He liked to stow a work by Shakespeare or another writer in his saddlebag to read in free moments.

A safari of this size was costly. To help pay expenses, Roosevelt wrote short articles about his excursion for *Scribner's* magazine. Andrew Carnegie, the former steel tycoon who now gave his money to worthy causes, also paid for the Smithsonian to send scientists on the trek.

The Smithsonian was just beginning to open large exhibition halls to eager visitors. It sent photographers to make a black-and-white record of the journey—and taxidermists to prepare the skins and bones of animals that Roosevelt killed for their exhibits back in the States.

Roosevelt liked to say he went on safari mainly to pursue his interests in studying nature. Much of what he shot ended up as dinner for the hunting party. Yet when Roosevelt lined up elephants, lions, and rhinos in his rifle sights, onlookers also noticed how much he liked to hunt for sport.

Sometimes what they saw displeased them. White hunters who lived in Africa had a set of unspoken but well-understood rules about big game hunting. They fumed when Roosevelt wasted ammunition or made wild, "ungentlemanly" shots. They condemned Roosevelt for overhunting, especially when he and Kermit killed nine white rhinos—adults and young of a nearly extinct species.

By the time his adventure ended, Roosevelt had shot more than 500 animals. His hunting party sent home to museums more than 11,000 animals, birds, and fish. Back at Sagamore Hill, Roosevelt kept a rhino's foot to use as an inkwell on his desk.

A photo montage showed the many faces of Theodore Roosevelt as his term as president ended in 1908.

Theodore Roosevelt on safari.
Library of Congress LC-USZ62-65500

Big Game Camera Hunt

WHEN THEODORE Roosevelt was living, fashionable gentlemen traveled thousands of miles across oceans, deserts, mountains, and jungles to hunt for exotic animals. They returned triumphant with animals' heads and skins, and often whole specimens stuffed as trophies for their homes. To Roosevelt's credit, the animals he shot and brought home mostly found their way into museums as displays.

There are animal-friendly ways to go on your own hunt for big game. Grab a camera and head out to the zoo. You'll find plenty of great targets for a good photo: elephants; big cats including lions, tigers, cheetahs, and leopards; primates such as gorillas, chimps, and orangutan; hooved creatures including rhinos, zebras, buffalo, and gazelles; and more.

You'll Need

- Piece of string about 4 feet long
- Small notebook that you can attach string to, such as spiral-bound or three-hole punched
- Camera
- Pen
- Your "pigskin" notebook (from page 3)

If you wish, you can arrange your visit by continent to discover which animals live there. Or you might focus on hunting only for prey with hooves or those with claws. A zoo map obtained online or at the zoo can help you plot out your hunt.

Use the string to tie the small notebook around your neck. Once you are at the zoo, follow your plan to check out the big game. As you snap pictures of your prey, take notes about their homelands. On which continent do they originate? What's their habitat? Are they endangered?

When you come home, print out pictures of your prize specimens and tape them into your "pigskin" notebook. Then enter some information about each. You can use a table like the one below.

BIG GAME NOTES

Name	Scientific Name	Homeland	Habitat	Foods	Endangered?	Notes
Bengal tiger	Panthera tigris	South Asia/Bangladesh	grassland and forests	meat	yes	"Bengal" means "Bangladesh

A Funeral and Fuss at Home

Kaiser Wilhelm II, Germany's leader, honored Theodore Roosevelt by inviting him to inspect German soldiers in 1910.

EDITH ROOSEVELT met her husband and Kermit in Egypt as they emerged from their adventures. The couple visited the capitals of Europe—Vienna, Budapest, Paris, Berlin, and Copenhagen. On May 5, Roosevelt stopped in Oslo to accept his award for the Nobel Prize that he'd received six years before for settling the Russo-Japanese War. Then a cable arrived from the U.S. government asking Roosevelt to attend a wake.

In England, King Edward VII was dead. True to tradition, the crowned heads of Europe were traveling to London for a magnificent state funeral. Kings, dukes, and princes swarmed a reception the night before hosted by Edward's son, the new king, George V. Roosevelt and a representative from France were the only men wearing formal suits and not fancy uniforms adorned with brass buttons and gold braid. Roosevelt's plain dress represented the clearest notion of what democracy meant.

As he journeyed through Europe, Roosevelt heard rumblings from home. Old-time Republicans, who did not back Roosevelt's reforms, were taking control of Congress. President Taft, though a kind, intelligent man, didn't have Roosevelt's skills to outsmart his opponents. It looked as though the country would back away from Roosevelt's progressive ways.

Taft also got into a bitter fight with Roosevelt's ally Gifford Pinchot and fired him from his job as head of the U.S. Forestry Service. Taft's acts disappointed Roosevelt; it seemed that he would not follow in Roosevelt's footsteps toward reform.

The Republican Party ripped in two over the issue of tariffs—taxes on goods imported from other countries. On one side stood the old-guard Republicans who liked the tariff because it helped businesses. Tariffs made imported goods more expensive, so U.S.

A Fate-Filled Funeral

No one who attended King Edward's funeral knew that this was a fateful gathering. King George V of Great Britain, Kaiser Wilhelm II of Germany, and Czar Nicholas II of Russia all shared a grandmother: Great Britain's Queen Victoria. In four years, these first cousins would be fighting each other across Europe and the Middle East in the Great War—what later became known as World War I.

In 1917, Germany, led by Kaiser Wilhelm, declared war on the United States. The next year, Kaiser Wilhelm would leave his throne in disgrace after losing the war.

In 1918, Bolshevik revolutionaries threw out the Russian government. They murdered the czar, his wife the czarina, and their five children. The Russian Empire was history.

businesses could charge high prices for their products, too.

On the other side was Senator Bob La Follette of Wisconsin, a progressive Republican who wanted to end tariffs. He liked the competition between foreign-made and U.S.-made goods. Americans would pay lower prices.

Roosevelt returned from Europe in June 1910. He looked forward to spending his summer at Sagamore Hill seeing his family and working at his new job as editor of *The Outlook*, a national magazine. However, the lure of politics overcame his ability to sit still.

In August, Roosevelt hit the road to take his progressive ideas to Americans. People everywhere clamored to hear him speak. The former president climbed into his bully pulpit to demand reforms, a New Nationalism. He called for a stronger central government in Washington. "This New Nationalism regards the executive power as the steward of the public welfare."

"The citizens of the United States must effectively control the mighty commercial forces which they have called into being," Roosevelt charged. Monopolies in business would always exist, but it was the job of the government to oversee them. Because state government refused to make those reforms, the federal government in Washington must.

Roosevelt also talked about the need for a graduated federal income tax. "The really big fortune, the swollen fortune, by the mere fact of its size,... [is different]... from what is possessed by men of relatively small means." Under his plan, very high earners would pay more taxes than people who earned much less for their labor.

Roosevelt's New Nationalism also called for careful conservation and development of the country's natural wealth. "I recognize the right and duty of this generation to develop and use the natural resources of our land; but I do not recognize the right to waste them, or to rob, by wasteful use, the generations that come after us."

Conservation, restrictions on child labor, fair pay for workers, controls on how businesses could donate to politicians—all were part of Roosevelt's cry for reform. Progressive Republicans loved him, but traditional Republicans despised Roosevelt's ideas.

Then Roosevelt attacked courts at the state level for favoring big business over the rights of working people. The solution, Roosevelt suggested, would be for citizens to have the right to vote judges off the bench in state courts. At that point, politicians in the middle worried that he was going too far, too fast.

The rumblings grew louder over the next two years. Roosevelt heard talk that maybe

Theodore Roosevelt's signature grin. Sagamore Hill National Historic Site, National Park Service

he, not President Taft, should be the Republican candidate in the next election. In their speeches, Roosevelt and Taft took aim at each other, and their friendship crumbled. By the time the Republican National Convention opened in June 1912, Roosevelt seemed far more popular than the president. But old-guard Republicans deftly blocked Roosevelt's delegates and returned the nomination to Taft.

COLONEL SAYS AGAIN FRAUD DEFEATED HIM roared the *New York Times* in August.

Theodore Roosevelt speaks at the Progressive Party Convention in 1912. Library of Congress LC-B2- 2495–9[P&P]

(After he left the White House, newspapers often called Roosevelt "Colonel Roosevelt.") But Roosevelt and those who backed him made plans to have a convention of their own in upstate New York. The *Times* reported early in September:

BULL MOOSE BOOMS, STIRRING UP STRIFE "Bull Moose" was Theodore Roosevelt.

The Election of 1912

NO LONGER a Republican but never a Democrat, Theodore Roosevelt ran for president on the Progressive Party ticket in 1912. Third-party candidates had appeared before in American politics, but none as strong as the Rough Rider. "[M]y hat is in the ring, the fight is on, and I am stripped to the buff," the bully candidate promised. Soon the new party was nicknamed the Bull Moose Party.

Roosevelt looked forward to a rousing campaign against Taft and Governor Woodrow Wilson of New Jersey, a college professor who was the Democrats' candidate. Like an excited cowman, he hit the campaign trail so that he could talk straight to the American people. Americans seemed to be just as excited to see their popular ex-president.

Roosevelt had been on the road just one week when he stopped in Milwaukee to make a speech. At 8:10 on the evening of October

14, Roosevelt slid into a car waiting to take him to a hall. He saw a thick crowd of well-wishers filling the streets in every direction, so he stood up and got out to take a bow.

"At this instant there cracked out the vicious report of a pistol shot," a friend reported. A would-be assassin hit Roosevelt in the chest. Two men jumped the shooter as Roosevelt steadied himself. He "again raised his hat, a reassuring smile upon his face, apparently the coolest and least excited of any one in the frenzied mob."

"He pinked me, Harry," the candidate said to his friend. With a bullet in his chest, Theodore Roosevelt rode to the hall and talked to the crowd for an hour and a half.

When an onlooker accused him of faking the shooting, Roosevelt opened his coat to show his bloody shirt. "It takes more than one bullet to kill a bull moose," he announced. He pulled out his speech, folded up in his shirt pocket. A hole ran through every page.

The doctors' report said the rest.

As the bullet passed through Col. Roosevelt's clothes, doubled manuscript and metal spectacle case, its force was much diminished. The appearance of the wound also presented evidence of a much bent bullet.... His condition was so good that the surgeons did not object to his continuing his journey in his private [railroad] car to Chicago where he will be placed under surgical care.

The rest of the presidential campaign of 1912 was a classic example of a three-party contest—with classic results. When votes were counted, it was clear that Roosevelt had wooed many Republicans away from Taft, resulting in a split Republican vote and a victory for Governor Wilson, the Democrat. Like Roosevelt, Wilson had campaigned for reform. As president, Wilson went on to see

The Progressive Party in America

President Roosevelt formed the original Progressive Party, known to most Americans as the Bull Moose Party, in 1912. It included people who pushed for reforms to improve conditions for everyday Americans. Progressives came from all walks of life, from farmers in the Midwest to working people in cities, from women who demanded the right to vote to others who wanted to outlaw alcoholic drinks. They asked for Americans to elect their senators themselves—this was handled by state assemblies at the time—and they also sought the right to remove corrupt officials in government. Progressives also took aim at corporate trusts and sky-high tariffs on imported goods. They hoped to stop child labor once and for all and to guarantee an income for the elderly. Progressives campaigned for pure-food laws to protect American families. The Progressive Party took various forms over the years and disbanded altogether in the 1950s. But many people today still define themselves as politically "progressive" in opposition to "conservative."

BUILD A DIORAMA

IN THE early 1900s, enchanted visitors flocked to museums to view exhibits and dioramas, giant scenes that showed stuffed animals and birds as they would appear in their own habitats. Theodore Roosevelt collected many such specimens on his travels through the American West, Africa, and South America.

You can make a diorama of any scene you'd like using a box and some materials you have around your home and in your kitchen. Just cook up some salt and flour dough to model your habitat, and let your imagination go wild.

You'll Need

- Pencil
- Paper
- Shoebox
- Paint
- Paintbrushes
- Building materials such as toothpicks, craft sticks, cotton balls, bits of cloth, etc.
- Salt
- Flour
- Water
- Deep bowl
- Food coloring
- Measuring cups and spoons
- Plastic wrap
- Found objects such as rocks, pebbles, shells, twigs, dried grass, etc.
- Miniatures of animals, birds, and people
- White glue

First, think about a theme for your diorama. What do you want to portray in this 3-D model? You can choose a habitat on earth—or maybe an otherworldly one. Will you create an indoor or outdoor scene? What colors will you use? Sketch out a plan on paper for your diorama.

If necessary, paint the inside of the shoebox.

Next, build any objects that will appear in your diorama, things like buildings, furniture, fences, or walls. Set them aside for a moment. Then prepare the landscape (for an outdoor scene) or backdrop (for an indoor scene) by following this recipe.

Homemade Clay

- 1 cup salt
- 1 cup flour
- ½ cup water
- Food coloring

Put salt and flour in the bowl. Mix the dry ingredients well with your hands.

Slowly add water and mix it in with your hands until you make dough. Knead the dough until it is smooth and elastic—kind of stretchy. Note: If you put flour on your hands before you start to knead the dough, you will find it less sticky to work with. If your dough turns out sticky, add a little more flour.

Divide the dough into several pieces and tint each one by kneading in one or two drops of food coloring. (Yes, food coloring will stain your fingers!) Keep each piece wrapped in plastic to prevent it from drying out.

Now you are ready to build your landscape/backdrop inside the shoebox. You can mold the salt dough any way you wish. If you run out, make more.

Before the dough is completely dry, add found objects to it. Special features such as rocks or cloth make your diorama come alive. Then glue in the pieces you have built.

Finally, it's time to populate your diorama with animals and/or people. What kind of stories can they tell?

that many of Roosevelt's progressive ideas made it into law.

But Theodore Roosevelt would have preferred to handle that task himself. Moreover, his bold break from the Republican Party lost him friends. As one friend who did stick by him recalled,

The telephone, which had rung like sleigh-bells all day and half the night, was silent. The North Shore neighbors who, in the old days, had flocked to Sagamore at every opportunity, on horseback or in their high fancy traps, did not drive their new, shining motor cars up the new, hard-surfaced road the Roosevelts had put in the year before. The Colonel was outside the pale. He had done the unforgivable thing—he had "turned against his class.

Surviving a River of Doubt

LOSING THE election stung Roosevelt, but things brightened when he left with Edith for South America the next October. Roosevelt's gifts in public speaking made him a sought-after guest, even in faraway spots such as Brazil, Argentina, and Chile. The trip south offered another prize: an adventure through uncharted lands in the Amazon River Basin.

The expedition, Roosevelt knew, offered him one "last chance to be a boy."

The Roosevelts bade good-bye to each other early in December 1913. Roosevelt, joined by Kermit and a Brazilian explorer named Candido Rondon, embarked on a journey across the Brazilian frontier and into the jungle. It was a scientific expedition. Their first goal was the source of the *Rio da Dúvida,* the River of Doubt.

Rondon suspected, but could not guarantee, that the river would carry them north toward the Amazon River and on to civilization. Rondon would map the unexplored river. Roosevelt's party of scientists would hunt and collect specimens of plants and animals for the American Museum of Natural History.

Roosevelt, Kermit, and the others took weeks just to reach the river. They passed through terrain as exotic and challenging as any Roosevelt had faced. When the party finally reached the River of Doubt, they split up. Some went back. Roosevelt, Kermit, and Rondon, together with other scientists and laborers, decided to stay the course. In seven dugout canoes, with the barest of equipment and food, the little group started down the River of Doubt.

Theodore Roosevelt had never thought of the wild outdoors as Mother Nature. "Of course 'nature'... is entirely ruthless... and works out her ends or no ends with utter disregard of pain and woe," he observed. On the River of Doubt, nature did not play favorites, and Roosevelt nearly died.

A series of horrific events nearly doomed the group. They lost five canoes in swirling rapids. One boatman drowned; Kermit nearly died, as well. Another boatman murdered a fellow worker. Those who were still left drove the guilty man away, into the jungle. The natives who stalked them were sure to kill him just as they had shot Rondon's dog: with a poison-tipped arrow.

Then Roosevelt himself took ill when he gashed his leg, opening the old wound from the long-ago carriage crash. Sick with infection, Roosevelt fought malaria and massive diarrhea, and his temperature rose to 105 degrees. He lay helpless in the middle of a canoe with his head propped up against a pile of cans. The crew fashioned a rough tent over his head.

Roosevelt urged Kermit and the rest of the group to leave him behind to die. He was prepared. Like many frontiersmen of the day, he carried a tiny glass vial filled with a deadly dose of poison. One crush of the vial with his teeth, and death would come in moments.

Kermit faced death from malaria himself, but he refused to leave his father's side. When the group had to bypass treacherous points in the river, Kermit helped his ailing father to hobble a few steps, sit for a rest, and hobble on.

Downriver, a group waited at the point where the River of Doubt flowed into another tributary of the Amazon. Finally, on April 26, Roosevelt's desperate party reached them.

Theodore Roosevelt points to a map of South America, showing his canoe trip along the River of Doubt.
Theodore Roosevelt Collection, Harvard University Library

Roosevelt had lost 55 pounds and could not walk, but he had finished his mission. Rondon had mapped the River of Doubt—all 1,000 kilometers (600 miles) of it. And Kermit had saved his father's life.

No sooner had Roosevelt returned home, weak from his journey, when criticism flared. Noted geographers did not believe that he had mapped an undiscovered river. Such a feat seemed impossible.

Angry, Roosevelt fought back. He gave a series of lectures about his adventures in the United States and sailed to England to meet members of the Royal Geographic Society. So weak his audience could barely hear him, Roosevelt described his monumental trek and pointed to a giant map that showed the Amazon tributary that he had traveled.

In Brazil the former president became a hero. The Brazilian government renamed the River of Doubt with its new title: Rio Roosevelt.

"The War to End All Wars"

ONE MONTH after Roosevelt returned from South America, the world changed forever. On June 28, 1914, the Archduke Franz Ferdinand of Austria-Hungary was assassinated as he visited the tiny country of Serbia in the Balkans. Austria-Hungary declared war on

STARGAZING BY SEASON

OF COURSE, the weather helped Theodore Roosevelt to know what season it was. Because Roosevelt spent so many nights camping under the stars, he understood why their position in the sky could tell him the season, as well.

Every night, you can observe constellations—groups of stars that form "pictures" in the sky. Just like the sun and moon, many stars appear to rise in the east and set in the west. As the earth spins, the backdrop of stars above our heads seems to rotate across the night sky.

Note: Something quite different appears in the northern sky. The Big Dipper and the Little Dipper, as well as the constellation Cassiopeia, seem to orbit Polaris, our "North Star." Can you think why?

From where we observe them in most of North America, these constellations are lower on the northern horizon. They do not seem to "rise and set."

Constellations change from season to season, but they follow the same pattern year after year. Summer, fall, winter, and spring, the parade of constellations over your head marches in the same order.

You can understand this concept with the help of two constellations. These star groups are Scorpius, a summer constellation, and Orion, a constellation that appears in winter.

Scorpius is named for the scorpion, an animal with a curved, stinging tail. The constellation Scorpius lies low in the southern sky. Look for its curving hook of stars.

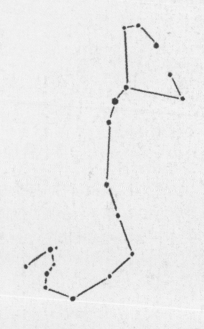

continued . . .

Orion, the hunter, is easy to find because of the three stars that form his belt. If you look closely, you can see another faint line of stars hanging from Orion's belt to form his "dagger."

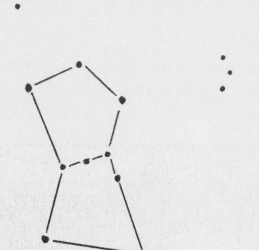

You can track the path of both constellations during an entire year—just not at the same time. With some planning and patience, your observations will tell what season it is just by looking up!

You'll Need

❖ Your notebook (from page 3)

❖ Pencil

❖ Star charts (See the NASA Web site at http://spaceplace.nasa.gov/en/kids/st6starfinder/st6starfinder.shtml)

❖ Compass

In your notebook, make a table like the one shown below.

Let's get started. You can begin your observations during any month except September and October. Make sure it is a clear night with a clear view of the sky.

What month is it? Visit the NASA Web site and print out the star chart for that month. Practice using the chart by holding it over your head, just as though you are looking at the night sky. Once you see how the chart works, you can look at it on a table.

(Note: The NASA chart has directions on how to fold it for a different use. However, you should keep it flat.)

Identify the location of Scorpius (or Orion) on the star chart. Scorpius is visible during June, July, and August. Orion is visible from November through April.

Now go outside and use the compass to find the southern sky. Look for your target constellation.

Enter your observations on the table in your notebook.

Think: why do constellations rise and set at different times each evening?

Stars rise and set according to the sidereal day, which is shorter than the "solar day" that we use to measure time.

MY CHART OF SCORPIUS JUNE–AUGUST (OR MY CHART OF ORION NOVEMBER–APRIL)			
Date	**Time**	**Position in Sky**	**Season**
June			
July			
August			

Serbia one month later. This declaration of war on one tiny country set the whole of Europe on fire. In days, all of Europe was at war.

In the early 1900s European empires were caught up in a tangled web of agreements called alliances. When one nation went to war, the other members of its alliance promised to join in. This is exactly what happened during the first week of August 1914. Once Austria-Hungary went to war against Serbia, Germany and Italy joined in on the side of Austria-Hungary to become the Triple Alliance. Italy dropped out, but the Ottoman Empire joined Germany and Austria-Hungary to become the Central Powers. On the other side, Great Britain, France, and Russia linked to become the Triple Entente, known later as the Allies.

No one could predict how fast the war became a nightmare of blood and death in the trenches of battle across Europe. In the United States, isolationists didn't see any need to enter a war thousands of miles across the Atlantic. Safe at home, Americans felt Europe's problems had little to do with them.

President Wilson spoke for many Americans when he declared that the United States would not take sides in the conflict. At home in Sagamore Hill, Theodore Roosevelt kept quiet about America's neutrality. In private, Roosevelt worried about the Germans' plans.

On his trip to Berlin, he had seen for himself the German government's hunger for power. Newspapers reported how the deadly German army had rolled over neutral Belgium on its way to invade France. Roosevelt felt certain that Germany was planning even more trouble that would catch the United States off guard.

He wrote to friends about the need for the United States to prepare for war. Just because a nation had its army and navy fully trained and equipped did not mean the country *had* to go to battle. As in the old days, the former

A bitter cartoon shows President Woodrow Wilson discovering Theodore Roosevelt's big stick in the White House attic. Wilson and Roosevelt disagreed loudly about the United States's place in World War I. Wilson wanted to use a "big stick" against Roosevelt. Library of Congress LC-USZ62-84054

president still believed that the United States should carry a big stick, ready to defend the nation.

However, isolationists still held the upper hand in America's foreign policy. Many progressives, as well as most Democrats, backed President Wilson's plans to stay neutral. In 1915 President Wilson even accepted Germany's apology after German submarines torpedoed the *Lusitania*, a British passenger ship, killing 1,959 people, including 123 Americans. Desperate to avoid conflict, most Americans believed that Germany would keep its promise to stop sinking non-enemy ships.

In the election of 1916, Wilson campaigned on the slogan "He kept us out of war," running against Republican Charles Evans Hughes. This election, the Republican Party would have nothing to do with Theodore Roosevelt. For his part, Roosevelt knew that the Bull Moose Party was dead.

Grateful Americans returned Wilson to the White House, and he kept to his official policy of neutrality. However, as news of German brutality poured in from Europe, more and more Americans began to side with the Allies.

At Sagamore Hill, Theodore Roosevelt waited like a lion sniffing the wind for trouble. On February 1, 1917, trouble came.

Americans Join the War

As 1917 opened, World War I had raged all over Europe and the Middle East for more than two years. President Wilson had offered several peace proposals to both sides, but no one came to a solid agreement to stop the war. Then, on February 1, Germany made a drastic decision. From that day forward, German submarines would feel free to torpedo most ships on the oceans, whether military vessels, merchant vessels, or all but a few passenger ships sailing in restricted zones.

On the heels of Germany's warning came another, when the British intercepted a telegram sent from Germany's foreign minister, Arthur Zimmermann, to the Mexican government. The telegram (which came to be known as the Zimmermann telegram) made it clear that if Mexico would harbor German submarines at its ports, Germany would support Mexico in an effort to take back Arizona, New Mexico, and Texas from the United States.

In March, Americans received yet another blow when German U-boats sank three American merchant ships filled with cargo. After meeting with his cabinet, Wilson's mood changed. Early in April 1917 the United States entered the war on the Allies' side to fight Germany and the other Central Powers.

Theodore Roosevelt could sit still no longer. For months, he and friends with like minds had drawn up plans to mount a division of volunteers to join the Allies in Europe. Such a force could be raised and trained within weeks, far ahead of what the regular army could hope to achieve. Roosevelt hurried to Washington to make his offer to Wilson. However, Wilson felt no sense of duty to a former president, who, like it or not, was a war hero. Wilson rejected Roosevelt's plan.

Roosevelt was furious. Here he sat, fit, trained, ready to serve his country, and the president had turned him down! The blood of the former Rough Rider boiled in his veins. Bitterly, he attacked Wilson for handling the war as "a cause for profound humility."

Sagamore Hill stayed a quiet place in 1917. All four of Roosevelt's sons were serving their country in battle. Ted and Archie had joined the U.S. Expeditionary Forces under General John Pershing, whom their father had known for years. Ted's wife, the "other Eleanor" in the family, left for France to work with the YMCA serving American fighting men. Kermit had gone off to Mesopotamia with British forces, and Quentin was learning to fly. Ethel and her husband, a doctor, were making plans to care for injured soldiers in France. Alice, in the Washington spotlight, watched as congressmen debated the war in their chambers.

Theodore and Edith awaited news from the front and treasured the letters that arrived from their children. Frustrated that he could not fight himself, Theodore took his thoughts directly to the American people. In the summer of 1917, he boarded a train for the Midwest, where he gave angry speeches about the country's weakness in the face of war.

He lashed out against "hyphenated" German-Americans who split their loyalty between their homeland and the United States. Yet at the same time, he called for immigrants from everywhere to receive equal treatment, based "upon the man's becoming in the very fact an American and nothing but an American.... There can be no divided allegiance here."

The old Rough Rider was ashamed at his nation's failure to be prepared for battle. "If the president had dared to lead, our people would have followed with eagerness and resolution; the long hesitation [about going to war] merely confused them and made them less unanimous when the time came."

Every week, Roosevelt wrote letters to his children. At every opportunity, he spoke with pride about his boys who fought and the Roosevelt women who did war work. Fortunately for the Roosevelts, the long days of waiting for war news were broken up with visits by friends—and a new generation. Ted,

A World War I poster urged American children to support General John Pershing in the war effort.
Library of Congress LC-USZC4-9559

Ethel, and Archie had presented Theodore and Edith with grandchildren. Again, the sound of small feet filled the halls of Sagamore Hill.

Theodore and Edith delighted in their role as grandparents. Theodore enjoyed spoiling his grandkids, these small persons, as he called them. He wrote amusing letters about their antics. One afternoon, they visited "that haven of delight, the pig pen."

I trundled Cornelius in his baby carriage while Gracie and Ted alternately carried and did battle over my long walking stick. We fed the pigs with elderly apples; then we came to a small rick of hay down which had to slide each of them in turn until I finally rebelled.

In many ways, Roosevelt felt helpless as he watched the United States blunder its way into battle. Still, the old soldier kept busy, railing at the government for the mess its training camps were in. Even the *New York Times* agreed. In an editorial, it declared "all our bustle and stir does not hide the fact that… we are far behind in our preparations to supply rifles, ammunition, machine guns, airships, uniforms, clothing for the troops."

Though Roosevelt rarely attacked Wilson directly, he blamed the president for poor

Theodore Roosevelt with two grandchildren. Library of Congress LC–USZ62-12

planning. Soldiers had poor equipment and sanitation: "broomstick rifles, logwood cannon, soldiers without shoes, and epidemics of pneumonia in the camps."

Christmas in 1917 passed quietly. With everyone at war, the family had only a tree for their young grandson. Alice wrote that her father's mind was on work. "I can see him sitting close to a lamp, a sort of triple-decker table crowded with books within easy reach, a fire blazing in the big fireplace in the north room. We did not have a gloomy Christmas— it simply was not Christmas at all."

In a snowy January week, Roosevelt journeyed to Washington to meet with members of Congress. Officials flooded Alice's home to hear him out. Plenty of Democrats were just as displeased as Republicans at how the United States had bumbled into war.

Journalists also flocked to hear Roosevelt speak at the Washington Press Club dinner. "Tell the truth," Roosevelt exhorted them. "If conditions are good, tell the truth. If they are bad, tell the truth. If they have been bad and become good, tell the truth."

The Republicans, who had scorned Roosevelt in 1912 and again in 1916, now listened to him. "Backbones stiffened," Alice noted, and they adopted his ideas at a party meeting. They agreed that party politics between Republicans and Democrats had

The Teddy Bear

Of the stories that arose during Theodore Roosevelt's life, the history of the teddy bear is best known. The tale began when a cartoon appeared in the *Washington Post* in 1902. The drawing featured President Roosevelt, decked out in his Rough Rider's uniform, refusing to kill a bear.

A cartoonist named Clifford Berryman drew the image after hearing about the president's hunting trip to Mississippi. For three days, the president and his hunting party had used dogs to track bears through the woods, without success. Finally, an aide found a bear, exhausted from being chased, and tied it to a tree for the president to shoot. But Roosevelt refused to kill an animal in such an unsporting way. (Sadly, someone else did kill the bear.)

Morris and Rose Michtom, a couple in New York, saw the cartoon. Morris and Rose were new Americans, Jewish immigrants who'd escaped

The "Cracker Jack Bears" No. 15.

bloody pogroms (organized killings) in Russia. By day, the couple ran a candy shop. By night, Rose sewed stuffed animals. Morris and Rose designed a small, sweet bear made with velvet and button eyes and put it in their window.

The toy bear was an instant success. Morris sent one to the White House, asking the president's permission to call it Teddy's Bear. Americans, enchanted with the story about their president, snapped up the Michtoms' toy bears as well as German versions made by the Steiff family.

Morris and Rose began manufacturing teddy bears full time and built their business into the Ideal Toy Company. By making the most of what they read in a newspaper, the couple wrote their own chapter of the American dream.

A popular postcard featured the Cracker Jack Bears to advertise the snack in 1915.

no place in wartime. Still, they agreed with Roosevelt that their patriotic duty was to criticize Wilson's men for a poor start to the war.

By the time he left for home, Theodore Roosevelt had regained the favor of the Republican Party. It seemed certain that he would run for president in 1920.

Needle Felt a Teddy Bear

NEEDLE FELTERS use raw, unspun wool, called roving, to shape all kinds of animals, human figures, and ornaments. Like human hair, the outer layer of a strand of wool is covered by overlapping scales called cuticles. By jabbing the wool with long, barbed needles, felters make these microscopic scales hook together. The more you jab a piece of raw wool with a needle, the firmer and more felted it becomes.

Would it surprise you to learn that needle felters like to make teddy bears? You can learn to needle felt a bear of your own with a little bit of practice and supplies that you buy at knitting stores or online.

Adult supervision required

You'll Need
- ❖ 2 large handfuls of wool roving in any colors you like (For beginners, coarse wool is easier to work with. Felting with fine wool such as merino wool is more difficult to handle.)
- ❖ 1 thick piece of foam rubber from an old pillow or purchased in a craft store
- ❖ Several felting needles—size 38 in a triangular shape
- ❖ 2 black peppercorns or small beads
- ❖ White craft glue
- ❖ Toothpick

When you are first learning how to needle felt, expect to spend some time practicing this art form. Felting needles are very sharp. You need to watch closely at all times so that you do not jab yourself. Always felt the wool using a thick foam-rubber pad.

To begin, tear a thin piece of wool roving about the size of a playing card from the mound of wool. Lay the roving on the rubber pad and begin to jab it gently with the felting needle. You don't need to jab the needle very hard or far into the rubber pad—just enough to get the cuticles on the wool to link together. After you have gotten the idea and feel of the felted wool, try concentrating your jabs in one area of the roving. Do you see what happens?

Now try rolling a piece of roving into a small ball and felt it. Then roll up another piece into a tube about the thickness of your finger and felt that. Are you getting a feel for felting?

Here's the cool part: you can join shapes together by felting them. Put the wool ball on the middle of the tube and jab the ball and tube all at once. Gradually, they will bond together.

When you think they are felted securely, overlap the ends of the tube and felt them together. You should end up with a ring.

Now you are ready to felt your teddy bear. Start with six pieces of roving. The largest piece will become your bear's body, and a second, smaller piece will work as its head. Four same-sized pieces will serve as arms and legs.

Teddy Bear Body

Take the first piece of roving that's about the size of your hand and shape it into a loose roll about the size of a toilet paper roll. To get a rounded shape, tuck in the ends of the tube.

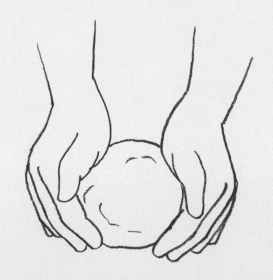

Start to felt your teddy bear's body by jabbing the wool all around the tube. Then you can begin to shape the body by using your fingers to mold the wool and needle felting it into place.

When you like the shape, and the wool is felted to the point where it no longer feels fuzzy and it holds its shape, set it aside.

Teddy Bear Head

Roll a piece of roving into a ball and needle felt it as you did your bear's body. Your teddy's head can be round or oval. If you wish, use your fingers and the needle to mold the head so your bear has a snout. Finally, you can create eye sockets by lightly punching the wool to create shallow depressions in its face. When done, set the head aside.

Teddy Bear Arms and Legs

Roll the four remaining pieces of wool into tubes about the thickness of your finger and felt them into arms and legs. With a bit of work, you can even shape the ends into paws.

Assemble Your Teddy Bear

Put all the pieces of your bear together by needle felting them into place. This is the time to make adjustments if you think something doesn't fit quite right, like an arm or a leg.

Add Details to Your Bear

To make teddy's ears, roll two tiny pieces of wool into small balls and felt them a bit. Then felt them to his head. Use the toothpick to dab his eye "sockets" with a tiny bit of glue and gently press a peppercorn or bead in each.

Think: when you pull on a strand of your own hair, why does it feel smooth in one direction and rougher in the other?

9

Living Life to the Hilt

IN 1918 the German army made its final thrust in France along the infamous line of battle, the western front. Thousands of American soldiers poured in to fight with France, Britain, and Belgium. All four Roosevelt sons were now in France. Ted and Archie had been wounded, Archie badly. Kermit had left the British and joined the Americans. Quentin earned his wings and joined a squadron of combat fliers. He "scored his first kill" against a German plane early in July.

About 10 days later, a reporter from the Associated Press paid a quiet call at Sagamore Hill and asked to speak to Roosevelt. Behind a closed door, Roosevelt read a cablegram that had been sent to the *New York Sun*. WATCH SAGAMORE HILL FOR—

Instantly, Theodore Roosevelt knew something had happened to one of his sons. He could account for Ted, Kermit, and Archie. Most likely, there was bad news about Quentin. But Theodore could not be sure, so during dinner and throughout the evening, he mustered all his bravery to hide the news from Edith.

The next morning, the reporter returned. His face betrayed his news. Two German fighters had shot down Quentin's plane behind enemy lines. Roosevelt's youngest child was dead.

"But—Mrs. Roosevelt! How am I going to break it to her?" Roosevelt asked, more to himself than to the reporter. He went indoors and told Edith the awful truth. Half an hour later, he came back outside with a statement for the press. "Quentin's mother and I are very glad that he got to the front and had a chance to render some service to his country, and show the stuff that was in him before his fate befell him."

The Germans buried Quentin with full military honors in a field close to where his plane crashed. Like other members of the Roosevelt family, Quentin was buried near where he died.

Mary Roberts Rinehart, a famous author of the day, went on an outing with the Roosevelts two weeks later. She noted that Theodore did not speak of his son, but Edith "spoke freely of Quentin, of how happy he had been the night before his plane was brought down, and that it had helped them to know that." Letters from Quentin had reached Sagamore Hill days after he died.

Rinehart offered a shrewd glimpse into Roosevelt's soul. "The war, to which he would so gladly have bared his own breast, had taken his boy and broken his heart instead."

The father spoke little about his son, but Roosevelt made clear his feelings in an editorial he wrote soon thereafter. It began, "Only those are fit to live who do not fear to die: and none are fit to die who have shrunk from the joy of life and the duty of life. Both life and death are part of the same Great Adventure."

Marching On

THEODORE ROOSEVELT marched on. Word arrived that Ted had been shot in the leg, while Archie, mustered out of the army, came home to rest. Once Ted recovered, he returned to the front as a lieutenant colonel, and Kermit joined him as an army captain. At Sagamore Hill, Theodore watched and waited for news. Wary as ever, he complained when President Wilson suggested that the war could end without Germany making a full surrender.

Quentin Roosevelt in his uniform. National Museum of the United States Air Force

Roosevelt held out hope that he could run for president in 1920. He left Sagamore Hill to make a rousing speech at Carnegie Hall in New York. On October 27 he celebrated his 60th birthday. He told his sister Corinne a secret: "I have kept the promise that I made myself when I was 21 . . . that I would work *up to the hilt* until I was 60, and I have done it."

Roosevelt compared himself to a swordsman. The blade on a sword runs from the tip to the hilt, the crosspiece that separates the blade from the handle. To work "up to the hilt" means to apply the same energy a knight uses to drive his sword into a foe.

On November 11, 1918, Germany surrendered unconditionally to the Allies, just as Roosevelt had hoped. The Great War, which most Americans thought was the War to End All Wars, was over.

That same day, Theodore went into the hospital, sick with inflammatory rheumatism. His leg and hand ached like never before. His body, never fully recovered from fevers and infections from his ordeal in the Amazon, began to betray him.

The ailing man stayed in the hospital for 44 nights. Edith slept in the next room. She went out to meet with friends and attend shows, returning with stories to tell her sick husband. At night, she read the plays of William Shakespeare to him.

For his part, Theodore worked from his hospital bed. On Christmas Day, his doctor finally allowed him to go home, where his grandchildren were waiting.

He continued to work from home, moving from his bed to an old couch in the children's nursery during the day. Friends came and went, and Edith got him outside for a ride now and then. Doctors promised that he would recover, but Edith expected that this would take time. She hired James Amos, Theodore's former personal assistant, to help care for him.

Theodore and Edith passed the afternoon of January 5 quietly. Quentin's girlfriend, Flora Whitney, visited him, and Theodore called in his secretary and dictated a letter to Kermit. Late in the afternoon, Theodore looked up at Edith and said, "I wonder if you will ever know how much I love Sagamore Hill."

That night, James Amos helped Theodore to bed. Edith looked in and saw him sleeping peacefully. She returned to her room, not wanting to disturb him. Amos sat in a chair keeping watch. In the dark hours of January 6, Amos heard a catch in the patient's breath. Theodore Roosevelt died in his sleep. A blood clot had traveled to his heart.

The next morning, friends and family gathered to mourn at Sagamore Hill. Archie

An engraving of President Roosevelt with the family crest below. Library of Congress LC-DIG-pga-03324

wrote a brief message and sent it to his brothers in France.

The cable read, THE OLD LION IS DEAD.

Life Goes On

EDITH ROOSEVELT lived out her days at Sagamore Hill—when she wasn't traveling. Edith became a globetrotter. In 1932 she spoke in favor of Republican Herbert Hoover for president against her nephew-by-marriage, Franklin Delano Roosevelt. She died in 1948 and is buried next to her beloved Theodore at Oyster Bay.

Alice Roosevelt Longworth stayed in the public eye until her death in 1980.

Ted Roosevelt married and had two children. He tried to enter politics but did better as a businessman. During World War II, Ted rejoined the U.S. Army as a brigadier general and commanded the Allied landing at Utah Beach in France on D-Day. He died of a heart attack days later. The family later moved Quentin's body so that the brothers are buried next to each other in the American cemetery in Normandy.

Kermit Roosevelt had a strained marriage with Belle Willard and fathered four children. He launched a steamship company after World War I. Like his brothers Ted and Archie, Kermit returned to battle during World War II. A victim of depression and alcohol, he took his own life while working for the army in Alaska in 1943. The family hid that fact from his mother.

Ethel Roosevelt married Dr. Richard Derby and was the mother of four children. Her oldest son, Richard, died of blood poisoning at age eight. Ethel was active in community life and much admired in Oyster Bay. She died in 1977 and is buried near her parents.

Archie Roosevelt married Grace Lockwood and fathered four children. A businessman, he returned to the Army during World War II, where he was cited for heroism in the Pacific. He was shot in the same knee that also took a bullet during World War I. He died in 1979.

In 1999 the United States returned the Panama Canal to the nation of Panama.

Today, Americans can visit five national sites that honor Theodore Roosevelt: his birthplace, his Badlands ranch, the home in Buffalo where he took the oath of office, Theodore Roosevelt Island in Washington D.C., and Sagamore Hill. All are held in trust for Americans by the National Park Service. They stand in tribute to Theodore Roosevelt, who as president set aside nearly one-fourth of the land in today's national parks.

Theodore Roosevelt's death mask.

Acknowledgments

I WOULD LIKE to thank my editor, Jerry Pohlen, as well as other fine people at Chicago Review Press for helping me bring Theodore Roosevelt's bully past to my young readers. I also thank the members of my writing group for their generous guidance as I wrote drafts of the book: Emma Berne-Carlson, Amy Hobler, Diana Jenkins, Kathy Kitts, Geri Kolesar, and Kellie Moster. And of course, to my husband, Bill, who's ready with a good cup of coffee and a kiss every morning.

Resources

There are many more ways to learn about Theodore Roosevelt's life and times. One of the best is to visit a library where you live and ask a librarian to help you.

Books to Read

THOSE TITLES marked with a ❖ are located in the children's or teens' department in the library or bookstore.

❖ Armstrong, Jennifer. *Theodore Roosevelt: Letters from a Young Coal Miner*. Winslow: 2000. (fiction)

Brinkley, Douglas. *The Wilderness Warrior: Theodore Roosevelt and the Crusade for America*. HarperCollins: 2009.

❖ Donnelly, Matt. *Theodore Roosevelt: Larger than Life*. Linnet Books: 2003.

❖ Fritz, Jean. *Bully for You, Teddy Roosevelt!* G.P. Putnam's Sons: 1991.

Hagedorn, Hermann. *The Roosevelt Family of Sagamore Hill*. MacMillan: 1954.

❖ Marin, Albert. *The Great Adventure: Theodore Roosevelt and the Rise of Modern America*. Dutton Children's Books: 2008.

McCullough, David G. *Mornings on Horseback*. Simon and Schuster: 1981.

Millard, Candace. *The River of Doubt: Theodore Roosevelt's Darkest Journey*. Doubleday: 2005.

Miller, Nathan. *Theodore Roosevelt*. Morrow: 1992.

Morris, Sylvia Jukes. *Edith Kermit Roosevelt: Portrait of a First Lady*. Coward, McCann & Geoghegan: 1980.

Roosevelt, Theodore. *Theodore Roosevelt, an Autobiography*. Charles Scribner's Sons: 1920.

❖ Whitelaw, Nancy. *Theodore Roosevelt Takes Charge*. A. Whitman: 1992.

Places to Visit

THE NATIONAL Park Service honors Theodore Roosevelt at five different locations you can visit.

Sagamore Hill National Historic Site

12 Sagamore Hill Road
Oyster Bay, New York 11771
(516) 922-4788
www.nps.gov/sahi/

Sagamore Hill welcomes visitors to Roosevelt's beloved family home. Rangers offer tours of the house, and guests can take nature hikes and picnic on the grounds. Special events are planned year-round.

Theodore Roosevelt Birthplace National Historic Site

28 East 20th Street
New York, New York 10003
(212) 260-1616
www.nps.gov/thrb/

Theodore Roosevelt's birthplace was rebuilt in the 1920s. Guided tours offer visitors a glimpse of rooms decorated in Victorian style, including the red velvet chair pictured on page 6 of this book.

Theodore Roosevelt Inaugural National Historic Site

641 Delaware Avenue
Buffalo, New York 14202
(716) 884-0095
www.nps.gov/thri/

Theodore Roosevelt was sworn in as president in this Victorian home. There are guided tours indoors and outdoor events on the grounds, including a yearly Teddy Bear Picnic!

Theodore Roosevelt Island

Turkey Run Park
George Washington Memorial Parkway
McLean, Virginia 22101
(703) 289-2500
www.nps.gov/this

Theodore Roosevelt Island sits in the Potomac River between Washington D.C. and Virginia. The park offers easy walking trails and a welcome escape from city streets. Visitors enjoy viewing wildlife on the trails and from a boardwalk over a swamp.

Theodore Roosevelt National Park

315 Second Avenue
Medora, North Dakota 58645
(701) 623-4466 (South Unit information)
(701) 842-2333 (North Unit information)
www.nps.gov/thro

This park is divided into North and South Units, with places to hike, camp, and view Roosevelt's Maltese Cross cabin. In the summer there are ranger walks, ranger talks, campfire programs, and trail rides available.

Index

Also available from Chicago Review Press

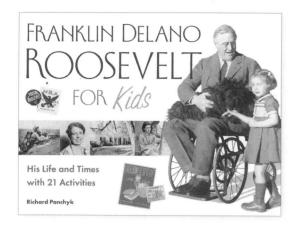

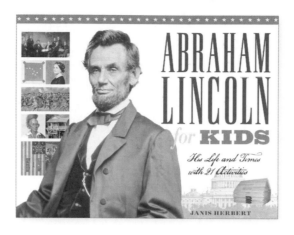

Franklin Delano Roosevelt for Kids
His Life and Times with 21 Activities
By Richard Panchyk

Ages 9 & up
Two-color interior, 60 b & w photos

Few presidents have left such an enduring legacy upon the history, culture, politics, economics, and art of this country as Franklin Delano Roosevelt. This book chronicles the Roosevelt family history, including famous cousin Theodore Roosevelt and first-lady Eleanor Roosevelt; FDR's early political career; and his 12 years in office that were some of the most fascinating and turbulent times in American history.

ISBN 978-1-55652-657-2
$14.95 (CAN $18.95)

Abraham Lincoln for Kids
His Life and Times with 21 Activities
By Janis Herbert

Ages 9 & up
Two-color interior, 100 b & w photos

"This original, informative, and entertaining book... should be required reading for every young person seeking a vivid introduction to Lincoln's life."

—HAROLD HOLZER, cochairman,
U.S. Lincoln Bicentennial Commission

ISBN 978-1-55652-656-5
$16.95 (CAN $18.95)

George Washington for Kids
His Life and Times with 21 Activities
By Brandon Marie Miller

Ages 9 & up
Two-color interior, 10 b & w photos, 50 b & w illustrations, 20 line drawings, 2 maps

George Washington comes alive in this fascinating activity book that introduces the leader to whom citizens turned again and again—to lead them through eight long years of war, to guide them as they wrote a new Constitution, and to act as the new nation's first executive leader.

ISBN 978-1-55652-655-8
$14.95 (CAN $18.95)

Available at your favorite bookstore, by calling (800) 888-4741, or at www.chicagoreviewpress.com

CHICAGO REVIEW PRESS

Distributed by
Independent Publishers Group
www.ipgbook.com

www.chicagoreviewpress.com